INCARNATION

MYTH OR FACT?

INCARNATION

△

MYTH OR FACT?

Oskar Skarsaune
Translated by Trygve R. Skarsten

Publishing House
St. Louis

Published originally as *Inkarnasjonen—myte eller faktum?* by Oskar Skarsaune. Copyright © 1988 by Lunde Forlag, Oslo, Norway.

Translated from the Norwegian with the permission of the publisher, Lunde Forlag og Bokhandel A/S, Oslo. Copyright Lunde Forlag in Oslo.

Copyright © 1991 Concordia Publishing House
3558 S. Jefferson Avenue, St. Louis, MO 63118-3968
Manufactured in the United States of America

Library of Congress Cataloging-in-Publication Data

Skarsaune, Oskar, 1946–
    [Inkarnasjonen—myte eller faktum? English]
    Incarnation—myth or fact?/Oskar Skarsaune; translated by Trgyve R. Skarsten.
        p.   cm.—(Concordia scholarship today)
    Translation of: Inkarnasjonen—myte eller faktum?
    Includes bibliographical references and index.
    ISBN 0-570-04547-9
    1. Incarnation—History of doctrines.   2. Jesus Christ—History of doctrines.
3. Jesus Christ—Messiahship—History of doctrines.   I. Title.   II. Series.
BT220.s4713   1991
232'.1—dc20   90-48939

---

1 2 3 4 5 6 7 8 9 10 VP 00 99 98 97 96 95 94 93 92 91

Contents

CONTENTS

Foreword

The Concordia Scholarship Today series explores current issues from a theological point of view and asks how the household of faith may meet the challenge to self-understanding that comes from the surrounding culture. The hope is that we may be able to comprehend more fully with all the saints what is the extent of the love of Christ toward all His creatures (Eph. 3:17–18).

Like all volumes in the CST series, *Incarnation—Myth or Fact?* offers insights at the level of theory that ultimately relate to current concerns, believing that a broadened and deepened understanding of the Christian faith will clarify and enrich our analysis of issues that beset us and in so doing help to "comprehend the love of Christ."

The CST series encourages Christians to think theologically about all matters of life. Exploration of an issue must grow out of reliable probing and research of the Scriptures and every other related, legitimate field of study. That may not always yield theological applications which differ markedly from the past. The greater value of such study lies in the learning process and in the assurance that the issue has been properly addressed.

Incarnation—Myth or Fact? probes the question, Who was Jesus? More books have been written about Jesus than any other person, and the debate still rages. Some believe there is no question. They accept by faith and without question the traditional Biblical answer: Jesus was God incarnate, the promised Messiah. For others, the question has no practical significance: Jesus could not be God incarnate. How they come to that position may differ, but in effect, theirs is a diminished, less than Biblical, concept of God and what that implies.

Between the two extremes are the genuine seekers, those who pose the question for a variety of reasons and with varying degrees of interest. This volume summarizes Oskar Skarsaune's thorough research on two related questions: (1) What was the Jews' concept of the Messiah and to what extent did Jesus meet their expectations? and, consequently, was Jesus really not God incarnate but only later made out to be so by the Jewish community? (2) Could the idea that Jesus was God incarnate have emerged from the Greek setting, and, once again, was Jesus not God incarnate but only considered so because of Greek religious thinking?

Obviously, the question is not merely academic and without implications. A theology that rejects the traditional view of the incarnation will be quite different from one accepting that view. If the possibility of incarnation is rejected, and if Jesus was not God incarnate, not only is the omnipotence and the very concept of God in question, there is no room for a substitutionary view of the redemption of humankind. The implications are far-reaching. At best, stripped of His deity, Jesus remains only an ideal role model. His resurrection and His power to perform miracles cannot be considered factually descriptive. One contemporary theologian, presumably following the existentialist Rudolf Bultmann, has accordingly rejected the reality of Jesus' resurrection ("the physical resuscitation of the corpse"), explaining that Jesus' disciples on Easter morning merely "met their future."

Incarnation—Myth or Fact? cannot provide final answers, nor can *any* research ever be absolutely definitive. Even the scientific world recognizes that nothing is empirically demonstrable beyond revision. Neither should Christianity, therefore, be subjected to a requirement of absolute verification. True, that Jesus is the incarnate Messiah is a matter of faith. Nevertheless, Skarsaune in this volume has demonstrated that faith in the incarnation of Jesus, the Messiah, can be more than simple trust in the Biblical account; it is also comprehendible and credible on the basis of rational research and study. Skarsaune's work nourishes and contributes to an inner consistency of a faith that is intellectually honest and defensible.

Dr. Trygve Skarsten, a respected scholar in this field, not only rendered the English translation but prepared a bibliography, which was not included in the original Norwegian edition, and has supplied numerous English titles.

The Publisher

Preface: A Little about the Book

This book grew out of eight lectures that I gave at the Independent Theological Faculty in Aarhus, Denmark, during January, 1986. I recall with gratitude the interesting and provocative gathering of students, faculty, and pastors with whom I was permitted to dialog. Later that year the Independent Theological Faculty published the lectures. The present work is a revised Norwegian edition [here translated in English].

In this edition, I have had in mind especially the kind of reader whom one in former times characterized as a "believing and searching student of Scripture." Theological jargon has been reduced to a minimum. The few terms that seemed unavoidable are explained in the glossary at the end of the book. A few Greek words are included in parentheses, but always in a way that the context makes their meaning clear. Endnotes are provided for interested theological readers, especially students. They contain citations from Early Church and Jewish sources, references to modern theological literature, and supplementary remarks of various sorts. The citations are at the end of the book so as not to disturb the more casual reader. One will not miss out on the main arguments or points of view if one elects to skip over the endnotes.

Everyone will not be familiar with all the persons encountered in a book such as this. Therefore I have introduced the most important names in boxes within the narrative of the text. A few of the boxes introduce important events and concepts.

I hope this will enhance the readability of this book for a much larger audience. I have been occupied for a long time with the issue discussed here. More will be said about this in the introduction. Let me just emphasize one thing here. I am painfully aware that this book deals with areas and source materials in which I do not dare call myself an expert. So be it. We theologians are accustomed to specializing narrowly in theology and often feel unsure of ourselves outside of the little acre we ourselves have plowed. However, the very theme of this book has compelled me to cover an area larger than my specialty. But I believe that the argument, overview, and attempt to see the larger relationship can be very fruitful. Nevertheless, the book will have to speak for itself.

I extend personal thanks to my colleagues at the Independent Theological Faculty [in Norway] for their inspiring professional attitude and warm personal support. Fellowship in the Collegium Judaicum has been especially meaningful for the ideas and views that have evolved in this book. The initial impetus for the book came from the annual lectureship of the Collegium Judaicum (later published in the Collegium's journal in 1977 under the title, "Treenighetslærens jødiske forutsetninger," pp. 3–12.) In addition, I owe thanks to the Norwegian Mission to Israel for two inspiring study leaves in Israel. The background and relationship within Judaism for a confession of Christ would hardly have played as large a role in this book had it not been for my contacts and the professional milieu at Hebrew University in Jerusalem and the many interesting conversations with staff and contact people at the Caspari Center. Finally, I want to extend a warm thank you to Jens Olav Mæland and the staff at Lunde Forlag, who took the initiative for this revised edition and who encouraged and supported me all along.

Oskar Skarsaune

Oslo
May 1988

Introduction: A Little about the Issue

In the beautiful countryside outside Caesarea Philippi, at the foot of Mount Hermon, Jesus asked His disciples two questions. The first was, "Who do people say that I am?"

Jesus was obviously interested to hear what people were telling the disciples about Him. The answers revolved mainly about the idea that He was undoubtedly a reincarnation of one of the great prophets, possibly John the Baptist or Elijah. It is amazing how modern these answers sound in our New Age era, that the spirit which had previously resided in Buddha, Zarathustra, and in the deepest consciousness of every individual dwelt in Jesus. Contemporary society today, steeped in its new religiosity, answers the question just about the same way. But that is an old answer. In the days of the Early Church, those whom we call Gnostics already fully developed this idea. The Early Church had to take the Gnostics into account in its confession of Christ, and it would indeed be strange if we could not learn something from the Early Church in this regard.

Just twenty years ago, a totally different answer was given to Jesus' question. For the generation of the sixties the image of Jesus had a focus completely different from the picture we meet today. But this view of Jesus raised new challenges for Christian theology. The problem was compounded because large segments of Christian theology had developed doubt and uncertainty about the church's traditional confession of Christ. Some wondered whether the confession of Jesus as Lord and Messiah among the first Christians actually had come from what Jesus thought and said about Himself. Others questioned whether the subsequent confessions about Christ—such as the Nicene Creed (A.D. 325)—were fully valid New Testament teachings about Christ. The answers to these questions relate directly to what one thinks about a seemingly totally different

11

problem, namely, the relationship between the Jewish and Greek world of ideas.

In this book I have tried to examine the relationship between these two questions. It has become an historical study in how the church developed its confession of Christ, and I believe it is an exciting story. Major emphasis has been laid on the first half of the story, on the first two centuries. But I wanted to tell more than a story. I wanted to examine the basis on which the confession of Christ rests. I see no reason to deny that for me personally it involves an existential question of faith. Jesus asked His disciples not only what people in general said about Him. But He asked a second question:

"And you, who do you say that I am?" We know what Peter answered on behalf of the disciples. In this book we will also look at the reply of the Early Church. But the question also comes to us, Who do we say that He is? Can we make Peter's answer ours? Can we make the answer of the Early Church ours? No historical investigation can remove the challenge or answer the question for us. But it can help us to see the alternatives more clearly and to see the foundation upon which the answers rest.

Something must still be said about the scope of the book. It is not meant to be a definitive examination of Christological creedal development. Rather the whole study is channeled quite narrowly through one concept or word, *incarnation*. This is a technical theological word and was already viewed as such in the Early Church. As far as I know, it was church theologians who coined the word. They needed a word to express something that was new already for the people of antiquity. The new concept is expressed in one pregnant sentence in John 1:14: "The Word became flesh and dwelt among us." Or still more succinctly in 1 Tim. 3:16: "He was manifested in the flesh" (Latin: *in carne*, from which *incarnation* is derived). The new concept was this: God's Son, who was with the Father from eternity, became a human being at a particular point in time and lived among us. For the people of that time, this was unheard of, an impossibility. For some modern theologians it is an expression of a hopelessly antiquated mythology. But both for that time and today, most will agree that this is the central content of the church's confession about Christ. This book focuses on that core.

The "Impossible" Dogma

The Impossibility of the Incarnation—From a Jewish Perspective

We begin with a citation:

> It was Paul who introduced and founded the Christian religion as we know it today. It was he who insisted that Jesus was divine and claimed that he was a prophet, anointed by his Lord Jesus.

This short citation contains a specific position regarding the origin of Christianity: Paul, not Jesus, founded Christianity and asserted the central doctrine of the Christian faith, namely, the doctrine of the divinity of Christ. Implied is that this faith was not founded by Jesus, that Jesus did not teach that he was divine. No, says the great liberal theologian Adolf von Harnack: On the whole Jesus did not preach about himself, nor did he place himself in the center of his message. Jesus' simple message was one about the mercy of God the Father. The Son for the most part had no place in it. Jesus' religion was a Father religion. Only later, and particularly with Paul, Jesus' simple message was transformed to a message *about* Jesus, a gospel *about* the Son. Jesus was a prophet and a teacher for the first eyewitnesses, possibly even their "messiah," who taught about the Father and the kingdom of heaven. But for Paul, he was God in human form who had come to earth to redeem his own creation.[1]

This point of view is considered very modern and radical, a product of modern historical-critical research, which arose in the last half of the nineteenth century. But it is not new at all. The text which I first cited above comes from a Jewish author who lived in the early Middle Ages![2]

But we can go still farther back. In Justin Martyr's *Dialog with Trypho the Jew,* written around A.D. 160, Trypho is depicted as saying,

> Those who affirm Him [Jesus] to have been a man, . . . and to have become Christ [the Messiah] appear to me to speak more plausibly than you who hold those opinions which you express. For we all expect that Christ will be a man [born] of men, and that Elijah, when he comes, will anoint Him. But if this man appear to be Christ, He must certainly be known as man [born] of men (*Dial.* 49.1. *ANF* 1:29).

Trypho is portraying his Jewish understanding of the Messiah: The Messiah is nothing more than a human being. He is not divine by nature but selected for a special mission in God's economy with Israel and the people. Justin, on the other hand, believes in Jesus as a divine Messiah who was with the Father before He became a human being, and who was born in a supernatural manner through a virgin. But Trypho dismisses this as a distasteful influence from Greek mythology.

> In the fables of those who are called Greeks, it is written that Perseus was begotten of Danae, who was a virgin. . . . You [Christians] ought to feel ashamed when you make assertions similar to theirs and rather [should] say that this Jesus was born man of men. And if you prove from the Scriptures that He is the Christ, and that on account of having led a life conformed to the law, and perfect, He deserved the honor of being elected to be Christ, [it is well]; but do not venture to tell monstrous phenomena, lest you be convicted of talking foolishly like the Greeks (*Dial.* 67.2).

Trypho gives a clear expression of Jewish messianic expectations. He casts aside any thought of a preexistent Messiah who dwelt with God and who was God. He also punctures a "modern scholarly" explanation as to how the idea of divine preexistence and a virgin birth arose: It comes from Greek mythology! Indirectly, Justin is admonished to "demythologize" his teaching about the Messiah. Only then can he be on an equal dialogical footing with Trypho.

Pinchas Lapide, a Jewish scholar in our own century, says basically the same thing:

> Paul brought the message of the Jewish Messiah to the pagan world with a commitment of complete faith. Earnestness overshadowed doubt. He was successful in being a Greek for the Greeks and a Jew for the Jews. He possessed courage to display religious imagination. He knew that he would be rejected if he

came either to Corinth or Rome and preached about an anointed Jewish Messiah who was David's son. They wouldn't understand what he was talking about. But for Greek and Roman ears, he would fare extremely well talking about an incarnate Son of God and a Logos, a divine Word who had descended in order to redeem the world. On the other hand, this made no sense to Galilean fishermen and shepherds. That was why Paul appeared in Jerusalem as a devout, faithful Jew proclaiming a Jewish Messiah, while for Greeks he spoke of a Savior who was the Son of God.[3]

Thus we are already dealing in the New Testament with two completely different and incompatible confessions about Jesus (two *christologies*). The first is a Jewish messianic confession in which the Messiah is nothing more than a human being like all of us, nevertheless *chosen* for His messianic role. The other is a Logos confession in which Jesus is depicted as a heavenly being who has come to earth to save humanity. The latter, unthinkable for Jews, represents an adjustment to Greek mythology.

Our two Jewish friends, Trypho from the second century and Lapide in our own, in essence say the same as Harnack (and the modern historical-critical school).[4] They all presuppose that a confession of Jesus as God's Word, the Logos, was an impossibility in a Jewish environment. On the other hand, they say that it was self-evident, yes, virtually unavoidable, in a Greek Hellenistic world. But is this correct?

The Impossibility of the Incarnation—From a Hellenistic Perspective

The available primary source material does not seem to support the idea that the concept of incarnation was without any problems in the Hellenistic world. Rather, it would seem that the Christian doctrine of the incarnation was just as much a stumbling block for the Greeks as for the Jews. True enough, the Greek gods supposedly could take on human form and appear in various roles on earth. But it is quite clear that those Greeks who really grasped what Christians said about Jesus understood that it was something completely different and equally as scandalous for them as it was for the Jews. It concerned antiquity's understanding of divinity.

When Christianity entered into the ancient world, Greek philosophers had for several centuries already directed a slashing critique against the gods of Homer's world and the dominant "myths" about the gods in general. That which the philosophers found especially scandalous and impossible about the mythological gods was their pronounced human, yes, excessive human character. Even to a greater degree than human beings, these gods were subject to suffering and often proved to be powerless over against the cunning and power of other gods. In contrast to this concept of deity, especially Platonic and Stoic philosophy developed an alternative, anti-mythological theology. God, or rather the divine, is far removed from human suffering and passion. God is "beyond suffering"; He cannot suffer. He cannot be subject to another's power. God is pure reason and absolutely sovereign. He is *apathês* (not suffering). Any human curtailment of God was unthinkable.[5]

By the first two centuries of the Christian era, this philosopical understanding of deity had become the common heritage of the cultured classes of Greco-Roman society. Both Jewish and Christian preachers could relate to this and employ philosophy as their ally in the struggle against the gods of paganism. But this involved a problem. Did not the anti-mythological, philosophical critique also undercut the Old Testament concept of God? Could the incarnation really be defended in the light of such an understanding?

We can take the church father Tertullian (ca. A.D. 200) as an example of how deeply this philosophical concept of deity penetrated even a Christian theologian's consciousness. Tertullian reads in the Old Testament about a God who appears on earth, talks with Adam in Paradise, eats in Abraham's tent (Gen. 18), speaks face to face with Moses (Num. 12:8), regrets that He has created human beings, etc. It is clear to Tertullian that these passages do not refer to God Himself. But how should one understand these passages that speak of God appearing on earth in visible form? Tertullian reasons as follows: It is axiomatic that God cannot be seen by human beings. Therefore it must have been *someone else* whom the patriarchs and prophets saw when they saw God. This someone else was the Son.

> Now then, He must be a different Being who was seen, because of one who was seen it could not be predicated that He is

16

invisible. It will therefore follow, that by Him who is invisible we must understand the Father in the fulness of His majesty, while we recognize the Son as visible through the dispensation of His derived existence, even as it is not permitted us to contemplate the sun, in the full amount of His substance which is in the heavens, but we can only endure with our eyes a ray (*Against Praxeas* 14.3).[6]

When God appears on earth in the Old Testament, it is always the Son who is referenced, since human feelings, reactions, and experiences attributed to God also pertain to the Son. That was the way the Son prepared for His incarnation, says Tertullian—partly by preparing God's people to believe that God in the Son actually would become human and partly by "practising" in His own person with these human emotions.

Even then He knew full well what human feelings and affections were, intending as He always did to take upon Him man's actual component substances, body and soul, making inquiry of Adam (as if He were ignorant), "Where art thou, Adam?"—repenting that He had made man, as if He had lacked foresight; tempting Abraham, as if ignorant of what was in man; offended with persons, and then reconciled to them; and whatever other (weaknesses and imperfections) the heretics lay hold of (in their assumptions) as unworthy of God, in order to discredit the Creator, not considering that these circumstances are suitable enough for the Son, who was one day to experience human sufferings— hunger and thirst, and tears, and actual birth and real death (*Against Praxeas* 16.2–5).[7]

Thus Tertullian has lessened the tension somewhat between the concept of God and the incarnation. He can say,

Whatever attributes therefore you require as worthy of God must be found in the Father, who is invisible and unapproachable, and placid, and (so to speak) *the God of the philosophers*; whereas those qualities that you censure as unworthy must be supposed to be in the Son, who has been seen, and heard, and encountered (*Against Marcion* 2.27.6).[8]

In light of the Hellenistic understanding of deity, these citations are clear evidence that the incarnation is an offense. And if these references are not enough, let me cite one more from Tertullian. After having written how the Son in the Old Testament "practised" taking on human characteristics, Tertullian adds significantly,

> Surely even these things could not have been believed, even about the Son of God, unless they had been given us in the Scriptures; possibly also they could not have been believed of the Father, even if they had been given in the Scriptures! (*Against Praxeas* 16.13)[9]

Considering such citations, it is not very convincing to speak of the early Christian milieu as one in which "incarnation thought" hung in the air and which inevitably called forth an incarnation Christology. If one does not consider Tertullian's philosophical difficulties proof enough, one can read Celsus, an enemy of Christianity who wrote a work against Christianity ca. A.D. 170.

> God is good and beautiful and happy, and exists in the most beautiful state. If then He comes down to men, He must undergo change, a change from good to bad, from beautiful to shameful, from happiness to misfortune, and from what is best to what is most wicked. Who would choose a change like this? It is the nature only of a mortal being to undergo change and remolding, whereas it is the nature of an immortal being to remain the same without alteration. Accordingly, God could not be capable of undergoing this change.[10]

> Either God really does change, as they (the Christians) say, into a mortal body; and it has already been said that this is an impossibility. Or He does not change, but makes those who see Him think He does so, and leads them astray, and tells lies![11]

> Dear Jews and Christians, no God or child of God has either come down or would have come down (from heaven)![12]

Celsus could say this with complete philosophical assurance, while at the same time he could maintain that one ought not despise the Greek myths, even if they spoke of the gods dwelling on earth. These myths are deep mysteries, says Celsus. He implies that the Christian belief in the incarnation is a gross misunderstanding of the intention of the myths.[13]

In light of this, it is highly presumptuous to insist that in a Hellenistic environment faith in Jesus as the incarnate Son of God nearly followed automatically, once the Gospel was preached.

Rather, the opposite was true. According to the primary sources, this preaching met with the strongest rejection by the Greeks.

Let me cite one more text. Augustine (ca. A.D. 400) says something of tremendous importance regarding the relationship between Greek thought and the dogma of the incarnation. It is true, says Augustine, that one can read in Platonic books much that is both correct and beautiful about the Logos of God.

> Therein I found, not indeed in the same words, but to selfsame effect, enforced by many and various reasons that "in the beginning was the Word, and the Word was with God, and the Word was God. The same was in the beginning with God. All things were made by Him. . . ." Furthermore, I read that the soul of man, though it "bears witness to the light," yet itself "is not the light; but the Word of God, being God, is that true light". . . . But that "He came unto His own, and His own received Him not. And as many as received Him, to them gave He power to become the sons of God, even to them that believed on His name"—this I did not find there. Similarly, I read there that God the Word was born "not of flesh nor of blood, nor of the will of man, nor of the will of the flesh, but of God." But that "the Word was made flesh, and dwelt among us"—I found this nowhere there. And I discovered in those books, expressed in many and various ways, that "the Son was in the form of God and thought it not robbery to be equal in God," for He was naturally of the same substance. But, that "He emptied himself and took upon Himself the form of a servant . . . and being found in fashion as a man, He humbled Himself, and became obedient unto death, even the death of the cross . . ."—this those books have not. . . . That "in due time, Christ died for the ungodly" and that thou "sparedst not Thy only Son, but deliveredst Him up for us all"—this is not there.[14]

I am of the opinion that Augustine has evaluated the Platonic writings quite correctly. For the people of antiquity, the concept of the incarnate Son of God in a crucified human being was not a simple or natural thought to grasp. Instead, the available primary source material points unambiguously to the incarnation as a great stumbling block and philosophical monstrosity which made it difficult to gain a hearing among Greeks and Romans. And as already indicated, the church fathers were themselves so philosophically conditioned that they felt its liability as well.

He who has but the smallest intelligence will not venture to assert that the Maker and Father of all things, having left all supercelestial matters, was visible on a little portion of the earth.

This citation does not come from Celsus, a critic of Christianity, but from the church father, Justin Martyr (*Dial.* 60.2).[15] It is meant to be taken seriously. Justin uses it as a decisive argument against Trypho who has claimed that it was God who revealed Himself to Moses in the thorny bush. As a good Greek, Justin dismisses this as absurd.

If anything can be clearly derived from the writings of the Early Church, it is the simple fact that the idea of incarnation was not self-evident in the Hellenistic world. Rather, the opposite was true. The inhabitants of the ancient world seem to have perceived with instinctive confidence that the Christian claim about Jesus was something qualitatively different from what the poets said about the gods of Homer—and was not only tasteless but philosophically impossible.

With great elegance Tertullian used this very point as an argument for the veracity of the dogma of the incarnation. He points out that the philosophical impossibility of the idea of incarnation—its, literally speaking, unthinkable tastelessness—is an indirect witness to its truthfulness. Because it is so unthinkable, it could not have been dreamed up. In other words, it could not have been *contrived.* But when it is still asserted, it can be for only one reason: The incarnation must actually have taken place. It must be from personal experience and irrefutable reality that Christians were led to postulate such an unthinkable idea. As Tertullian says against the heretic, Marcion, who denied the incarnation,

> To be sure, other things are also quite as foolish (as the birth of Christ), which have reference to the humiliations and sufferings of God. Or else, let them call a crucified God "wisdom." But Marcion will apply the knife to this doctrine also, and even with greater reason. For which is more unworthy of God, which is more likely to raise a blush of shame, that God should be born, or that He should die? that He should bear the flesh, or the cross? be circumcised, or be crucified? be cradled, or be coffined? be laid in a manger, or in a tomb? . . . You will not be "wise" unless you become a "fool" to the world, by believing "the foolish things

of God.".... The Son of God was crucified; I am not ashamed of it. And the Son of God died; it is by all means to be believed, because it is absurd. And He was buried, and rose again; the fact is certain, because it is impossible![16]

My point is simply this: In the ancient world the Christian dogma of the incarnation was considered to be unique and especially offensive. Insightful critics of Christianity clearly recognized that they were not dealing with a common variant of a mythological theme. They were being confronted with something that collided head-on with their concept of divinity. The church fathers themselves contribute the decisive argument that this was the case: The incarnation also caused them difficulties because they shared the same concept of divinity.

This then is the big question: Can an environment that considers the dogma of the incarnation to be a philosophical absurdity simultaneously produce such a dogma? I believe that this question remains a legitimate point in Tertullian's line of argument cited above, namely:

How Could Faith in the Incarnation Arise?

A point of view that seems to be gaining in scholarly research is that the oldest incarnation texts of the New Testament are not Hellenistic but Jewish. It means that if one is going to understand the concept of incarnation historically, one needs to understand that it has arisen in a Jewish[17] environment in which one was accustomed to differentiate sharply between the Creator and the created (cf. Rom. 1:25).

This can be illustrated from a well-known episode in Acts 14:11–15. Paul and Barnabas had healed a man in Lystra.

> And when the crowds saw what Paul had done, they lifted up their voices saying in Lycaonian, "The gods have come down to us in the likeness of men!" Barnabas they called Zeus, and Paul, because he was the chief speaker, they called Hermes. And the priest of Zeus, whose temple was in front of the city, brought oxen and garlands to the gates and wanted to offer sacrifice with the people. But when the apostles Barnabas and Paul heard of it, they tore their garments and rushed out among the multitude, crying,

"Men, why are you doing this? We also are men, of like nature
with you, and bring you good news, that you should turn from
these vain things to a living God who made the heaven and the
earth and the sea and all that is in them."

One could certainly cite this text as evidence that incarnation
lay close to the thinking of many people. But if one looks closer at
the text, one sees that the Lycaonian expressions are not genuine
incarnation statements, but statements about gods in disguise: "The
gods have become *like* human beings." If the Lycaonians had had
the opportunity to read John 1:14, they no doubt would have reacted
with great bewilderment, just as other people did in the ancient
world. The point is, the background setting for incarnation thought
is not represented by the polytheistic Lycaonians but by Paul and
Barnabas! At the thought of being considered divine, Paul and Barnabas reacted with the Jewish response to blasphemy: They slashed
their cloaks! Among *such* persons belief in the incarnation arose
and found its first expression. In one way or another, we must be
able to render a trustworthy historical explanation of this phenomenon or else we have not really explained it.

From this perspective, belief in the incarnation and the teaching
of it becomes a tremendously exciting research topic. One could
first ask, Was belief in the incarnation less offensive in a Jewish
environment than in the Greek? The answer must seem to be an
unambiguous no. Even more pointedly, Was it not virtually impossible for incarnation thought to exist in a Jewish milieu which differentiated so sharply between God and the world, the Creator and
the created, and was so jealously observed and directed? One has
then to ask the same question that we posed with regard to the
Hellenistic world: Can a Jewish environment, in which the thought
of incarnation is practically impossible, at the same time be the
source for such a doctrine?

By asking such questions I have no doubt already implied that
obviously (at least for me) the doctrine of the incarnation cannot
be explained at all just by referring to a certain milieu. To put it
another way, we will not go to some "early primitive congregation"
or to a later form of Christianity to discover the origin of the dogma
of the incarnation. We must go further back, to the disciples' experience of Jesus Himself. In one way or another, through being

with Jesus, the conviction that Jesus burst all known categories of Judaism must have been impressed upon the disciples. This assertion obviously needs to be defined more adequately and developed, but for the moment, I will let it remain as it is. To sum up and conclude: It is not possible to explain the doctrine of the incarnation by simply stating that such a belief was practically self-evident in either a Jewish or Greek environment. Nor is it correct to say that this doctrine could have arisen when people thought mythologically but that it has become impossible for us, since we do not think mythologically. True, the Greeks were accustomed to myths about gods who walked upon the face of the earth. Yet, in spite of that, or perhaps because of it, they reacted with strong, instinctive conviction when they encountered the proclamation, *the Word had become flesh*. This is completely different from what is said in myths. This is unprecedented.

Proclaiming the incarnate Son of God was controversial and challenging from the very beginning. In no environment was it considered natural or self-evident. That pertained both to people who were steeped in mythological thought and those who were not. Thus we have to look for something completely other than mythology when we ask how this proclamation came about and how this doctrine arose.

2

The Incarnation in the New Testament

An Incarnate Messiah?

"You are the Christ, the Son of the living God" (Matt. 16:16). "God has made Him both Lord and Christ, this Jesus whom you crucified" (Acts 2:36). These statements of Peter leave no doubt that both Matthew and Luke regarded Jesus as Messiah to be the basic Christian confession. Their designation of Jesus as *Christ* is itself sufficient for us to assert that both authors were correct. *Christos* is the Greek for the Semitic Messiah, "the anointed One," whom God had promised. The first disciples were convinced of this and proclaimed Him as such to their Jewish compatriots.

But this poses a problem. Does this Messiah-confession relate to faith in the incarnation and, if so, how? We have already alluded to Trypho the Jew's rebuttal to Justin:

> Those who affirm Him [Jesus] to have been a man, and to have been *anointed by election,* and then to have become Christ, appear to me to speak more plausibly than you [Christians] who hold those opinions which you express. For we [Jews] all expect that Christ will be a man [born] of men, and that Elijah, when he comes, will anoint him. But if this man appear to be Christ, he must certainly be known as man [born] of men (*Dial.* 49:1, emp. added).[1]

What Trypho is here saying seems to be supported generally by contemporary Jewish sources: The Messiah is expected to be a royal son from the line of David and the royal line goes from father to son. Not only does any thought of preexistence or incarnation seem to be unknown but is directly excluded by Jewish thought.[2] It almost seems impossible that the oldest Christian congregation [Jerusalem]

24

could itself have evolved a dogma of the incarnation because the first disciples were Jews and were thoroughly steeped in their Jewish environment. At a bare minimum we can say that there was nothing in the inner dynamic of the oldest [pre-Jesus] Messiah-confession that would call forth an incarnation-faith. It is therefore not surprising that many scholars in the 1970s were convinced that Christian belief in the incarnation arose (relatively speaking) *later* than the Messiah-confession and that it had to arise on Greek soil or at least in a heavily Hellenistic form of Jewish Christianity.[3] As stated previously, I believe that this position is also untenable.

Incarnation Christology: Preexistence and Creator Agent

We now look more closely at incarnation Christology in the New Testament.

Only a single verse, John 1:14, speaks *directly* about the incarnation. Other references are indirect statements about Jesus' preexistence and sometimes are juxtaposed with His work as a person. For the moment we will leave "John's Prologue" (John 1:1–18) and group together some other texts relating to preexistence and incarnation:

> For us there is one God, the Father, from whom are all things and for whom we exist, and one Lord, Jesus Christ *through whom are all things* and through whom we exist (1 Cor. 8:6).

> He is the image of the invisible God, the first-born of all creation; for *in Him all things were created,* in heaven and on earth, ... *all things were created through Him and for Him.* He is before all things, and *in Him all things hold together.*... He is the beginning, the first-born from the dead, that in everything He might be preeminent. For in Him all the fulness of God was pleased to dwell, and through Him to reconcile to Himself all things, whether on earth or in heaven, making peace by the blood of His cross (Col. 1:15–20).

> But in these last days He has spoken to us by a Son, whom He appointed the heir of all things, *through whom He also created the world.* He reflects the glory of God and bears the very stamp of His nature, *upholding the universe by His word of power.* When He had made purification for sins, He sat down at the right hand of the Majesty on high (Heb. 1:2–3).

The words of the Amen, the faithful and true witness, *the beginning of God's creation* (Rev. 3:14).

A quick perusal of these texts is enough to arrive at an important point: In these passages the concept of Christ's preexistence has a decided shape. Nothing is said about a preexistence that assumes the preexistence of the human soul (as some of the Jewish scribes—and Plato also—held); nor is there any thought of the Messiah as a resurrected David or an incarnated heavenly angelic form. These ideas (and anything similar) are foreign to the above texts. The explanation is simple: The central thought in them is that Christ *assisted in creation.* For short, let us speak of Christ as a *partner in creation.* The preexistent Christ was the *agent* in creation. The texts assume a Christ who stood outside of and was preexistent to creation. It is this to which the texts speak directly and which we wish to address.

For the background to this concept of a preexistence one should not go rummaging through every possible philosophy that deals with preexistence for some or all humans or even for the Messiah. Instead one should ask, Where do we find the concept of a personage who functioned as God's assistant, as a partner in creation, when God created the world? Acknowledging that this is the correct question, the answer is not difficult to find. In both the Old Testament and the Old Testament Apocrypha, *the Wisdom of God* is spoken of precisely as an agent of creation.

Keep in mind the distinctive point already seen in the Old Testament and which evolves further in later Jewish literature. The wisdom of God, the Spirit of God (they are sometimes identified), the name of God, the glory of God, and the Word of God—all these terms can at times be used *as though referring to a person.* This applies especially to the wisdom of God (hereafter with a capital W). It can even appear as an eloquent "first person" alongside of God. (Citations from various texts will follow later).

It is no doubt correct to say that scholars do not know exactly how to respond to this phenomenon. Some prefer to speak of *poetic personification* of certain aspects or characteristics of God. But in several texts Wisdom seems to appear as an autonomous person, so that it is not sufficient to speak just of poetic personification.[4] Other scholars propose therefore to speak of an *hypostasizing* of certain attributes of God—without making us any more the wiser. (Regarding *hypostasis,* see p. 81). For our purposes, we need not come to a definitive conclusion about this difficult question. What is all-important is that the moment the discussion about the Wisdom of God was transferred *to Jesus,* the discussion of Wisdom as a person took on a totally new shape.

Look now at some of the numerous statements in Scripture and the Apocrypha where Wisdom is referred to as a participant in creation or where Wisdom speaks directly about the matter:

> The Lord *by wisdom founded the earth* (Prov. 3:19).
>
> [Wisdom says:] When He assigned to the sea its limit, . . . when He marked out the foundations of the earth, *then I was beside Him like a master workman* (Prov. 8:29–30).
>
> For she is an initiate in the knowledge of God, *and an associate in His works* (Wisdom of Solomon 8:4).
>
> *And by Thy wisdom hast formed man,* to have dominion over the creatures Thou hast made. . . . With Thee is wisdom, who knows Thy works and was present when Thou didst make the world (Wisdom of Solomon 9:2, 9).

The citations from the Wisdom of Solomon, one of the Old Testament Apocrypha books, comes from a Greek-speaking Jewish author in Alexandria around 200 B.C. But it was not just among Greek-speaking Jews in this Hellenistic metropolis that the concept of Wisdom's cooperation in creation was known. Among the rabbis of Palestine, the concept played just as great a role. They found it in the Hebrew text of Gen. 1:1, where they read, "In the *beginning,* God created the heavens and the earth." And who or what is the *Beginning?* They found the answer in Prov. 8:22 where *Wisdom* says, "The Lord created [or perhaps better, *gave birth to*] me as the Beginning." In other words, the Beginning is none other than Wisdom, so that Gen. 1:1 can read: "Through Wisdom, God created the heaven and the earth."[5]

Because the concept of cooperation in creation is so exclusively tied to Wisdom, the statements concerning *Christ* as an agent in creation do not necessarily have their background in the concept of Wisdom. However, it can be supported through two other observations.

First, there is a striking similarity *in the phraseology and expres-*

sions between Wisdom and the preexistent Christ. See, for example the following comparisons:

Heb. 1:3	Wisdom 7:26
He *reflects* the glory of God and *bears the very stamp* (*charakter*) of His nature.	For she is a *reflection* of the eternal light, a spotless mirror of the working of God, and an *image* (*eikon*) of His goodness.
Col. 1:15–17	Wisdom 7:26
He is the *image* (*eikon*) of the invisible God	[For she is] an *image* (*eikon*) of His goodness.
	Prov. 8:22–23
the *first-born of all creation*	The Lord *created* [gave birth to][6] me *at the beginning* of His work. . . . I was set up, *at the first,* before the beginning of the earth. . . . *When there were no depths,* I was brought forth.
	Gen. 1:1 and Prov. 8:22
He is *before all things* (*the Beginning*).	Wisdom is *the Beginning* through whom God created the world.[7]

The other item that undergirds this parallel between Wisdom and Christ is that some texts speak about a sort of "incarnation" of Wisdom in which Wisdom is said to come down from God's heaven to dwell in Israel. The two best known texts are found in the Old Testament Apocrypha, Sirach (ca. 190 B.C.) and Baruch.

> I came forth from the mouth of the Most High, and covered the earth like a mist. I dwelt in high places. . . . Among all these [people] I sought a resting place; I sought in whose territory I might lodge. Then the Creator of all things gave me a commandment, and the one who created me assigned a place for my tent. And He said, "*Make your dwelling* in Jacob. . . ." In the holy tabernacle, I ministered before Him, and so I was established in Zion. In the beloved city likewise He gave me a resting place, and in Jerusalem was my dominion (Sirach 24:3–11).
> Who has found her [Wisdom's] place? And who has entered

her storehouses? . . . Young men have seen the light of day, and have dwelt upon the earth; but they have not learned the way to knowledge [Wisdom] nor understood her paths. . . . Their sons have strayed far from her way. . . . God did not choose them, nor give them the way to knowledge [Wisdom]. . . . Who has gone up into heaven, and taken her, and brought her down from the clouds? Who has gone over the sea and found her and will buy her for pure gold? No one knows the way to her or is concerned about the path to her. But He who knows all things knows her. . . . He found the whole way to knowledge [Wisdom] and gave her to Jacob His servant and to Israel, whom He loved. Afterward *she appeared upon earth and lived among men.* . . . [8] All who hold her fast will live, and those who forsake her will die. Turn, O Jacob, and take her; walk toward the shining of her light. . . . Happy are we, O Israel, for we know what is pleasing to God (Baruch 3:15–4:4).

(In the Sirach citation, I have italicized the close parallel to John 1:14: "And the Word became flesh and *dwelt* among us.")

It is my contention that we must go to the Old Testament Jewish understanding of Wisdom if we wish to find the background of the New Testament statements about the preexistent Christ as an agent of creation. (This position is neither new nor original. On this point, recent scholarship has approached virtual unanimity.[9]) But this presents two fundamental questions that demand answers if we are to present a faithful historical account of the origin of Christology. First, What precipitated the identification of Jesus and Wisdom? What caused people to conclude that Jesus was the Wisdom of God to whom the Scriptures and tradition testified? Second, What is the relationship of wisdom Christology and messianic Christology? Are these two entirely different concepts, or is there some inherent connection between Messiah and Wisdom? We look at the first question.

The Concept of Wisdom in Judaism[10]

In the Old Testament we meet Wisdom as the *creative thought of God.*[11] This became an important concept during the Intertestamental Period when Jews were confronted with an entirely new challenge—the challenge from Hellenistic culture. The legacy of

Plato had great significance for Greeks, especially his notion of the visible world being a depiction of the spiritual world (usually spoken of as Platonic "idealism"). Timeless spiritual "ideas" are seen as the foundation for the visible world. Stoicism, another important Greek philosophy, saw no division of the world into material and spiritual. All reality was material. Stoic philosophy did, however, see the Logos at the center of the physical world, a sort of "world reason" that governed and gave the world shape and form, an inner law which guided the universe. A person's highest duty was to conduct his or her life so as to conform to this world reason. In a similar manner, the Platonists taught that an ethical life is a reflection of the idea of "good" in the spiritual world. In both cases, an ethical life was considered to be one in which a person *sought wisdom, loved wisdom (sofia)*—in other words, a life filled with the "love of wisdom," *filio-sofia.*

Thus Greek philosophy contended that *it* had insight into the ground of being of one's existence and insisted that it had discovered a universal ethic applicable to all people. A Jew who followed the commandments in the Decalog must have appeared very peculiar and different to Greek philosophers. In fact, we have evidence that many Jews themselves in the Intertestamental Period found the Law an ever increasing problem, because it isolated them from their environment and was difficult to substantiate philosophically.[12]

This was the challenge to which the authors of the Book of Sirach and the Wisdom of Solomon directed their attention. It also explains why the apocryphal Book of Wisdom became so important for them. To these authors, the "general plan" from which the world was created, the "world reason" which constituted the foundation of law in the world and which gave rules for the good life was none other than the Wisdom of God. The one who desires "to seek wisdom," to become a "philosopher," that person ought to seek *this* wisdom, God's wisdom! To make sure that it wasn't a question of any kind of wisdom but rather the Wisdom of the only true God who alone could dispense it, both authors identify this Wisdom with the Law. Sirach states this explicitly in chapter 24 (which we have already read):

All this is the book of the covenant of the Most High God, the law which Moses commanded us as an inheritance for the congregations of Jacob (v. 23).[13]

In the Wisdom of Solomon, the identification occurs more indirectly (e.g., 6:4, 18; 18:4). But the author leaves no doubt whatsoever that true Wisdom, which people cannot find by themselves and which is dispensed only by God to those who ask (7:6ff), has been given to Israel and to Israel alone. Here the author of the Book of Wisdom expresses a new and important concept which we can perceive in other intertestamental literature. The Wisdom by which the world was created and which is God's creative thought *was also active in the salvation history of Israel and is itself that history's creative power* (chaps. 10f).

> A holy people and blameless race wisdom delivered from a nation of oppressors. She entered the soul of a servant of the Lord, and withstood dread kings with wonders and signs. She gave to holy men the reward of their labors; she guided them along a marvelous way, and became a shelter to them by day, and a starry flame through the night.[14] She brought them over the Red Sea, and led them through deep waters (10:15–18).

In this and other passages we meet the idea that Wisdom, God's creative thought, was not only active when God created the world but was also active *in Israel's history*. Indeed, the tenth chapter of the Wisdom of Solomon speaks explicitly about Wisdom leading the people of Israel out of Egypt, going in front of them and behind them while in the desert. Interestingly, Wisdom is spoken of in a manner similar to how Paul speaks of Christ in I Cor. 10: "The Rock which followed them was Christ."

Thus Wisdom becomes the entity *which holds creation and salvation history together*. The God of creation, who with His Wisdom created the world, also broke into history with that same Wisdom. His Wisdom "found its dwelling-place in Zion" and "wandered among humankind." The God *of creation,* who is also the Lord *of history,* uses His Wisdom as His "agent of implementation."[15]

It is not difficult to see how effective this Jewish answer was to the challenge of Hellenism. Israel's election and subsequent history, the commandments and regulations which make her a holy people, unique and different from all other people, are not strange, odd, or unreasonable, but are derived from the same Wisdom who is the

31

architect and artist in the work of creation. It is not the Greek lovers of wisdom, the philosophers, who have discovered the world's reason and learned from it eternal precepts. It is Israel who has received the wisdom which is both God's own creative thought and internal plan of creation. Other people do not recognize this. They view the pious Jew as a miserable crank and deride his reference to being a child of God (Wis. 2:10ff; 5:3ff). In spite of the fact that it might appear otherwise, the Jew knows that life itself is to be found in God's wisdom, in a life lived according to the Law and that on the great day of visitation all this will be made plain. Then the one who has lived according to Wisdom will win life and receive a share in the royal kingdom which God promised humanity on the day of creation (Wis. 2:23; 3:7f; 5:15ff).[16] Through Wisdom, humanity will be saved (9:18)—just as Jacob already received a glimpse of God's kingdom from Wisdom (10:10).

Wisdom thus becomes the common denominator for creation, salvation history, and salvation itself. That it is a Jewish concept of wisdom that we are dealing with and not a Hellenistic one is most clearly seen in the furious polemic against idolatry that is contained in the latter half of the Wisdom of Solomon (12ff). Wisdom is to cleave to the God of Israel, the Creator of the world. The worship of Egyptian idols is folly itself.

Interesting and especially noteworthy is that, when Wisdom is used in this manner as an overarching concept for the whole of salvation history, Wisdom is also included in temple worship and the high priest's atoning work (Wis. 18:20ff). Wisdom comes to Zion from her heavenly "tent"(Sirach 24:4) and tabernacles there. "In the holy tabernacle I ministered before Him" (24:10). This corresponds to the listing in chapters 44–50 of the heroes of salvation history who join in a hymn of praise of the high priest Simon ben Onias and his temple service (Sirach 50:1–28).[17]

In Sirach and in the Wisdom of Solomon, we see only the beginning of an initial identification of Wisdom and the Law.[18] It would become more pronounced as time went on, and in later rabbinic theology the roles would be reversed, with Law replacing Wisdom as the dominant concept. But, without question, this early identification of Wisdom and Law left permanent impressions in the rabbinic understanding of law. The Law was thought of as being preexistent, as an agent of creation and the primal plan according to which the world was created. All of these are motifs earlier associated with Wisdom. As a well-known rabbinic commentary on Prov. 8:30 and Gen. 1:1 states,

> The Law says, "I was the worktool of the Highest, praise be to Him!" Among human beings when a king builds a palace, he does not build it according to his own design but according to the architect's. The architect does not build it ad hoc out of his head but uses plans and drawings so that he can see how the rooms and doors should be situated. So also with God: *He went according to the Law and so created the world.* For the Law says, Through the Beginning God created. The Beginning is none other than the Law as it says in the verse: "The Lord created me as the Beginning" (Prov. 8:22).[19]

As Maimonides, the great Jewish teacher from the Middle Ages, correctly observed, Plato expressed himself in the same manner when he said that God "sees" the world of ideas and from them creates visible objects (with the ideas serving as models).[20] In rabbinic Judaism, the Law thus becomes the overarching concept that holds together creation and salvation history, creation and election, creation and commandment, creation and redemption. A life in accordance with the Law is a life lived in accordance with the fundamental plan of creation itself.

Jesus and Wisdom

Against this brief summary background of important elements in Jewish wisdom literature, we now turn to Christology and ask, Why did Jesus become identified with Wisdom? Or, more directly, Was there something about Jesus' own behavior that gave rise to this identification? To examine this question more closely, it may be useful to ask, What for a *modern* Jew is peculiar about Jesus' preaching? Many Jewish scholars today hold that it is not the *content* of Jesus' preaching in and of itself that sets Him apart and differentiates Him from other rabbis of His own time. What distinguishes Jesus is the manner in which *His own person,* His own *I,* manifests itself. The Swedish rabbi, Marcus Eherenpreis, speaks insightfully about this matter:

> A difference [between Jesus and the Jewish rabbis] appears

immediately that from the very beginning constituted an un-bridgeable wall of separation between Jesus and the Pharisees. Jesus spoke in his own name. Judaism, on the other hand, knew only one *I*, the divine *Anochi* (the Hebrew word for *I*) who gave us the eternal commandments at Sinai. No other superhuman *I* has existed in Judaism other than God. Jesus' sermons begin, "I say to you." The prophets of Israel introduced their preaching, "Thus says the Lord." Here is a clash that goes to the inner core of religion. Jesus' voice had an alien sound that Jewish ears had never heard before. For Judaism, only the revealed teaching of God was important, not the teacher's personal ego. Moses and the prophets were human beings encumbered with shortcomings. Hillel and his successors sat where Moses sat. Every learned scholar is a link in an unbroken chain of tradition that stretched from Moses to our own time. Jesus seemingly snaps this chain and begins a new one. A man arose in Israel who cried, "I say to you." This was the new and strange element that arose between Jesus and the Pharisees.[21]

The manner in which Jesus said *I* appeared peculiar and dif-ferent. This point is so important that we must look at it more carefully. Was it unheard of in the Judaism of Jesus' time for a person to speak a word from God by his authority and command? Certainly not.

To begin with, the Jews knew "the prophets" who spoke directly from God. Even though many believed the time of the prophets had passed and that one had to abide by the prophetic books from the "classical" period of the prophets, few on principle denied the pos-sibility of a new prophet arising. Moses had promised that such a one would come (Deut. 18). Most of the people seemed to have great expectations for such a "prophet." John the Baptist was asked if he was "the prophet." Many no doubt placed Jesus in the same category.

For that matter, the rabbis also spoke words from God when they defined how the Law pertained to Israel. The Jewish scholar, Jacob Neusner, has shown in a very striking manner how a rabbi [one learned in the Law] was given an authority that came close to making him into "the personification of Law" or "the Law as a person."[22]

But there was never any lack of identification or clarity con-cerning the bounds of this position. Common to both the prophets and the rabbis was the understanding that they were only *spokesmen* or *representatives* for God and His Law. The prophets emphasize their role as messenger or representative by the so-called messenger formula, "Thus says the Lord." The prophet speaks and acts not in his own name, but in the name of God, who has commissioned him. He points to the whole time behind himself, back to God. The prophet does not have God's Word *in* him so that it becomes his own. No, it "comes to him." He receives it and passes it on. Through the word that he proclaims, the prophet will seek to bring his hearers into a relationship with God, not into a relationship with himself. In short, the prophet is a *representative* of God.

The rabbi is even one step further from God as His representative. The rabbi cannot even speak "in God's name." He does not say, "Thus says the Lord"; the most he dare say is, "Such is the Law." He undergirds his utterances by reference to the tradition of Law, to his predecessors, his teachers. Rabbi C says, "I have received as tradition from Rabbi B who heard it from Rabbi A. . . . "

Jesus, obviously, was not this kind of a teacher of the Law. He never undergirded His statements in this way. Instead, He set His own personal *I* against the whole tradition of the Law, the Mosaic legacy being no exception. "You have heard that it was said to the men of old. . . . but *I* say to you. . . ." (Matt. 5). For Jewish ears, this must have sounded shocking. They must have asked, "Who are you to dare set your own authority against Moses, who wrote down the Law from God's dictation! The Law belongs to God. Who are you to set yourself above it in your own name?" According to the evangelists, people were beside themselves, wondering about Jesus because He taught *with authority,* not as the rabbis.

Nor was Jesus a prophet [in the classical Old Testament sense]. He was called a prophet by many and could speak indirectly of Himself as a prophet. But He never used the prophet's "trademark," the messenger formula, "Thus says the Lord." Rather, He said, "*I* say to you. . . ." While the prophets and John the Baptist pointed away from themselves to God, Jesus said, "Come to *Me,* you who labor." Or, as He said to the disciples, "Follow *Me.*" He also spoke differently about martyrdom than folks were accustomed to hearing. The Jews were prepared for martyrdom for *the sake of God* or for *the sake of the Law.* But Jesus admonished His disciples to be prepared for martyrdom for *His* sake.

In a well-known book, *Jesus the Jew,* Geza Vermes states that the category of prophet best describes Jesus.[23] Vermes is thinking not merely about Jesus' preaching but foremost about Jesus' authority when He healed the sick and drove out demons. There was, says Vermes, a charismatic tradition in Judaism which granted that special spirit-endowed persons could have gifts of healing and other awe-inspiring capabilities. As examples, Vermes points to two well-known characters in rabbinic literature: Honi, "the Circle Drawer" (in the first century before Christ) and Hanina ben Dosa (who lived about the same time as the apostle Paul).[24] However, comparing these two with Jesus, more differences than similarities come to mind. Both Honi and Hanina are seen primarily as great *reformers.* Honi gets his nickname "the Circle Drawer" from a famous story in which he drew a circle on the ground to induce God to let it rain, but no rain came. Then he drew a circle on the ground around himself and said to God, "I will not move out of this circle until You have been gracious to Your children." *Then* the rain came![25]

Honi did not possess a divine word that could direct the forces of nature, but he could *ask God* for rain. The Jewish exorcists could do likewise. They themselves did not possess any power to scare away the demons. They had to receive this power from outside themselves through prayer, exorcism, and magical rituals. They also invoked a litany of "powerful" names, especially those of God and Solomon.[26]

Jesus was different. He did not heal through prayer but through His powerful command. He did not "receive" power before He drove out the spirits; He did it with a simple, powerful word that was His own. He did not ask God to still the storm and calm the waves; He did it with His own word. Though only God could forgive sinners, Jesus did it—and He underlined His power to do so by giving notice that He could also speak God's creative word, "Rise, take up your bed and walk"!

If one first recognizes this emphasis in the evangelists' portrayal of Jesus, one can see also that it is characteristic of the oldest "layer" of the gospel accounts. It is found in the common deposit of the gospels and in the most widely diverse material in the gospels. The evangelists can also expound on other characteristics. Luke, for example, can portray Jesus as a man of *prayer* and a spirit-endowed *prophet.* The evangelist John includes the statement that Jesus could not do anything except it be the will of His Father—as though John felt it necessary to underscore this because Jesus spoke and acted so mighty and sovereign![27]

To pull the threads together: Jesus appears in roles and functions that burst all previously known categories in Judaism.[28] He was a prophet but more than a prophet. He was a teacher but taught with a power and authority completely unknown to the rabbis. He could set His authority alongside of, yes, even "over" God's authority in the Law. He could utter words with creative power. In a Jewish environment zealous for the Law, only one category was "large enough" to contain this description of Jesus: the category of Wisdom.

Wisdom shared in God's creative word. Wisdom knew the secrets of the spirit world, and it was through Wisdom that Solomon had power over the spirits (according to Jewish tradition).[29] As we have seen, Wisdom is identified with the Law. When Jesus says, "You have heard it said [in the Law] but *I* say to you. . .", He does not receive His authority from the Law but speaks as though He were that very authority that also speaks through the Law. The rabbis could say, "Take the yoke of the Law upon you. God will then give you rest."[30] Jesus said, "Come to *Me*, all who labor and are heavy laden, and *I* will give you rest. Take *My* yoke upon you, and learn from *Me*; for *I* am gentle and lowly in heart, and you will find rest for your souls. For *My* yoke is easy, and *My* burden is light" (Matt. 11:28–30).

According to my understanding, there can be no doubt that Jesus conducted Himself in a manner that made it impossible to avoid identifying Him with Wisdom. The sovereign authority with which Jesus conducted Himself towards the Law could not be understood and accepted in a Jewish society zealous for the Law unless it was recognized that Jesus belonged within the same theological category as the Law—or, better yet, that *He* was the one who rightfully belonged there and that the Law had to be understood through Him, not the reverse. But then Jesus would have to be understood as the one who embodied God's whole plan of salvation. In the same manner as Wisdom and Law had previously done, He had to unite creation and redemption, creation and regeneration, in His own person. He who said *of Himself* what was usually reserved only for Wisdom or Law could not be understood as anything less than the incarnation of Wisdom.[31]

New Testament belief in the incarnation must be understood against this Jewish background. It was the only possible conclusion to the historical Jesus' contention that He was the absolute authority over against all other authorities. In short, He insisted that *in His person* He was the authority of the Law.

One more thing: As previously emphasized, the Jewish concept of Wisdom had also come to involve temple worship, yes, even its expiational aspect. When Jesus, functioning through His words and acts, entered into the role of the Law, sacrifical atonement was central to that Law (Matt. 5:23–24). If Jesus was to be the embodiment of the Law and the Wisdom of God for His people, it was not so unthinkable that the Wisdom of God had to include the folly of the cross. Then it becomes understood that He who had the characteristic of Wisdom and upheld the world through His powerful word (Heb. 1:3) also had to be our rightful high priest.

This concludes our preliminary answer to the first question, Why was Jesus placed in the category of Wisdom? Next we look more closely at the question, How does wisdom Christology relate to messianic Christology?

Messiah and Wisdom[32]

First, an item of a more general nature.

I believe that Christian scholars often misinterpret first-century Jewish messianism in one particular respect: That Judaism must have assumed a messiah with certain functions, so that salvation in the messianic age would be tied directly to the Messiah Himself and to His work—i.e., that the salvific age would be built around the Messiah as savior. That assumption of what first-century Jewish messianism believed is, in all likelihood, very misleading. The dominant concept in Jewish eschatology is messianic age or political state, not the Messiah. In fact, some writings from the last two centuries before Christ herald the time of salvation without even mentioning a messianic king.[33] Describing the messianic age in theater terms, one might expect the messianic characters (on stage or in the wings) to determine the action. But there is no such clear-cut design in the various documents or among the various groups of that time. Rather, the drama as a whole determines the image of the eschatological players, who they are and what they do.[34] With the knowledge we now have regarding how complex and pluralistic Judaism was in Palestine before A.D. 70, we should be wary of reading New Testament Christology as if it had a Jewish *messianology,* unchanging and locked in place. Rather, there is every reason to suppose that the portrayals of Messiah were quite different and varied considerably, even though they were drawn from a common overall eschatological concept.

Our primary source material for Palestinian Judaism during the first seventy years of the Christian era is very sketchy, more meager than we often recognize. All the rabbinic material (including that about the Messiah) was written down much later but has often been used uncritically as evidence for Palestinian Judaism before A.D. 70. Therefore its uncritical use has been a misuse.[35] On the other hand, we have an outstanding source of Jewish messianism in the first century in a book which we have examined so closely that we no longer recognize it from this point of view: the New Testament itself. I believe Christian scholars are all too reluctant to utilize the direct and indirect testimonies to Jewish messianism which the gospels contain. More directly, I maintain that one is completely justified in asserting that, where the gospels clearly seem to present a concept as alive during Jesus' lifetime, we have every possible reason to believe that such was the case, even if we lack other contemporary Jewish data to substantiate that concept. The gospels are themselves, from this point of view, just as good "Jewish" documents as any other.

The above general observations will no doubt become more concrete as we examine two concepts central to the connection between messianic Christology and wisdom Christology: the "Son of Man" (a term we meet in the Ethiopic Book of Enoch's "Similitudes," chaps. 37–71); and Solomon as a possible model for the messiah.

> *The Ethiopic Book of Enoch,* a Jewish work, consists of several smaller books, most from the first century after Christ (though some are older). In several of the books that make up this work, Enoch is presented as one who has received

a glimpse of heaven and who therefore can be a conduit for revelation. Large sections of the Book of Enoch do sound like John's Book of Revelation. Chapters 37–71 (the Similitudes) are considered by most scholars to be the most recent section, no doubt written about the time of the New Testament. Large sections of the Book of Enoch, but not the Similitudes, are found in the Aramaic text among the Dead Sea Scrolls.

In the Similitudes, we encounter a visionary figure called "the chosen one" (45:3, 4; 49:2, 4; 51:3, 5; 52:6, 9, *et al*) and God's "anointed" (48:10; 52:4).[36] With characteristics directly taken from Isaiah 11 (e.g., 49:3f), we are no doubt here presented with a messiah-figure, whose work is described in messianic terms:

> He shall depose the kings from their thrones and kingdoms.
> For they do not extol and glorify him [God], and neither do they
> obey him, the source of their kingship (46:5).[37]

He is a messiah, however, a very special messiah. The content of the Book of Enoch is crucial: He "whose face was like that of a human being"(46:1) reveals himself to be no one else other than the beholder himself, Enoch. And like the Enoch of Genesis, *he is a wisdom-figure:*

> In him dwells the spirit of wisdom, the spirit which gives
> thoughtfulness... (49:3).
> In those days (the Elect One) shall sit on my [his?] throne,
> and from the conscience of his mouth shall come out all the secrets
> of wisdom... (51:3).[38]

One can perhaps say that wisdom is "incarnated" in this Enoch-messiah. Not that the two are so closely identified that the words of creation are attributable to Enoch (that would no doubt have been considered an intolerable deification), but "the Elect One" *is* said to have a kind of preexistence:

> Even before the creation of the sun and the moon, before the
> creation of the stars, he was given a name in the presence of the
> Lord of the Spirits (48:3).[39]
> For this purpose he became the Chosen One; he was con-
> cealed in the presence of (the Lord of the Spirits) before the
> creation of the world, and for eternity (48:6).[40]

His messianic work embraces an aspect that is barely touched on in the Old Testament messianic prophecies but which is important in the structure of the Enoch literature:

> Kings, potentates, dwellers upon the earth: You would have to see my Elect One, how he sits in the throne of glory and judges Azazel and all his company, and his army, in the name of the Lord of the Spirits (55:4)![41]

Here we encounter a messiah figure who clearly has wisdom characteristics and whose messianic work includes a judgment over the demons under Azazel's leadership. The point is not that this messianism forms a direct background for the gospels' picture of Jesus as Messiah. The point is rather that the Similitudes reveal some of the background for Christians to shape a messiah figure in the first century of the Christian era.

We now proceed to a brief consideration of the Solomon figure. It is manifestly evident that Solomon is not just any ordinary figure when one is discussing wisdom Christology, because he plays the role of author in large sections of the wisdom literature (Proverbs, Ecclesiastes, Wisdom of Solomon). He is, for example, the *I* who is the speaker in the Wisdom of Solomon and who explains how Wisdom came to him and dwelt with him (chaps. 7–8). Because of his participation in Wisdom, he received insight into the "power of the Spirit." This theme later plays a large role in the character of Solomon, in popular literature[42] as well as in the rabbinic legends.[43] In the Testament of Solomon he is depicted as a great exorcist. Josephus views him in a similar manner.[44]

Since Solomon was David's son, it is quite possible that thoughts about him could reflect and transfer over to the designation "son of David," used as a messianic title for Jesus (Matt. 9:27; 12:23; 15:22; 20:30f; 21:9).[45] The disciples (and/or the suppliants for help) fall back on this designation when they see Jesus heal and are impressed by His power over the evil spirits. Jesus does not reject this title but instead claims it by saying that judgment upon those who do not believe in Him will be severe:

> The queen of the South will arise at the judgment with this generation and condemn it; for she came from the ends of the earth to hear the wisdom of Solomon, and behold, something greater than Solomon is here (Matt. 12:42).

41

The same "one-upmanship" of Solomon is built into the words that Jesus could rebuild the temple in three days. Solomon was, above anything else, the temple-builder who, according to rabbinic legend, built the temple with the assistance of the spirit. "Something greater than the temple is here!" (Cf. Matt. 12:6).

The Solomon-theme can also be pursued through other citations—e.g., in Psalm 89 the words about the son of David are partly transferred to David himself, probably in his capacity as a prototype for the eschatological son of David. Note also Nathan's promise to David (2 Sam. 7:11b–16; 1 Chron. 17:10b–14; Ps. 89:4, 20–38), which alludes to David's son with reference to Solomon (2 Sam. 7:12–14), as well as to an eschatological son of David (1 Chron. 17:11–14). Several important themes are contained in Nathan's promise: (1) David's son will call God *father,* and God will call him *son.*[46] (2) God will "raise up" this "son." I agree with those exegetes who here see the background for the messianic confession found in Rom. 1:3 ". . . designated Son of God in power . . . by His resurrection from the dead."[47] (3) This "son" shall be installed as king in the "kingdom of God" (1 Chron. 17:14: "I will confirm him [David's son] in My house and in My kingdom for ever"); cf. 2 Chron. 9:8; 1 Chron. 28:5. In 2 Chron. 13:5 there is talk about the "God of Israel [who] gave the kingship over Israel forever to David and his sons."[48]

Let me underscore two points. First, Jewish messianism during the time of Jesus included considerable "openness" regarding various viewpoints. Paramount no doubt was the understanding of a national messiah who would either throw off foreign domination or who would interpret the Law (as in rabbinic expectations). But there also was a lively expectation of a messiah who, in combination with Wisdom, would destroy demonic power and usher in the Kingdom of God.

Second, we must not forget that, for the first disciples, belief in Jesus as Messiah was based primarily on faith in Jesus' resurrection and enthronement at the right hand of the Father. This point can be seen in the New Testament texts which seem to presume that Jesus "embarked" on His real messianic work through the resurrection (cf. Acts 2:36) and which therefore also entitle Jesus as the messianic Son of God precisely because of His attribute as the Resurrected One (cf. again Rom. 1:3f).[49] The texts imply that, as the Resurrected and Enthroned One, Jesus from the very beginning had to break the ingrained rabbinic messianism. As we have seen, in all probability elements for such a sundering had already been visualized before the resurrection. I believe that the gospels' portrayal is historical when reporting a "Messiah-secret"—which the disciples presume but which they also partly misunderstand—and their *wonder* and fear of Him whom even the wind and the waves obeyed. But it was the assurance of Jesus' resurrection that provided the final answer for their suspicions and wonder. That answer had to include both a confession of Jesus as God's Messiah and a confession of Him as the Lord through whom the world was created, who was Lord of both the living and the dead. It was no Hellenistic myth but rather the encounter of the disciples with Jesus before, during, and after Easter, together with the background material which their Judaism gave them, that brought about the very early Christian confession of God's Messiah who in the beginning was with God and who was God, and who took upon Himself flesh and dwelt among us.

Let me quickly summarize this chapter. We began by stating that the usual Jewish portrayal of the messiah (such as we find in rabbinic literature) does not as a matter of course lead to a personal preexistent or incarnated Messiah. For the background of the texts that speak of Jesus' preexistence and incarnation, we are led to the Old Testament and Jewish documents which discuss the Wisdom of God. We found that the behavior of Jesus caused Him to be placed in this category: He acted with an authority and power that can only be understood if He is the incarnated Wisdom of God. Finally, we said that even if the usual Jewish messianism did not seem "to demand" a preexistent, incarnated Wisdom in the role of Messiah, there are Jewish documents which reveal a messianism "open" to this direction. When the oldest confession to Jesus confessed Him to be both Messiah and the incarnation of Wisdom, it was a juxtaposition that could at least be understood in a Jewish environment where the first [Christian] proclamation was heard. The final and deciding factor with regard to this juxtaposition lay not in the expectations or demand of the people but rather in Jesus' own person and in His behavior.

3

Incarnation Thought during the First Two Centuries

The Offense of the Cross

For since, in the wisdom of God, the world did not know God through wisdom, it pleased God through the folly of what we preach to save those who believe. For Jews demand signs and Greeks seek wisdom, but we preach Christ crucified, a stumbling block to Jews and folly to Gentiles, but to those who are called, both Jews and Greeks, Christ the power of God and the Wisdom of God. For the foolishness of God is wiser than men, and the weakness of God is stronger than men (1 Cor. 1:21–25).

This well-known Pauline passage draws attention to two concepts placed opposite each other, as though in counterpoint, representing respectively the primary points at issue for Jew and Greek. Jews seek *signs* as they await a *strong* Messiah. They take offense at the *weakness* of the crucified. But those who do believe see the power of the crucified God. The Greeks seek *wisdom* and dismiss the gospel of the crucified as *foolishness*. But precisely in this foolishness the wisdom of God is hidden.

This juxtaposition readily recalls something quite characteristic of Judaism (and Hellenism) in its reaction to the message of the crucified Messiah and Son of God—a reaction reflected in Trypho's words to Justin:

These and similar Scriptures [Dan. 7:13 etc.] compel us to wait for him [Messiah] who, as Son of man, receives from the Ancient of days the everlasting kingdom. But this so-called Christ of yours was dishonorable and inglorious, so much so that the last curse contained in the law of God fell on him, for he was crucified[!] (*Dial* 32:1).[1]

This had also been the Pharisee Paul's conclusion with regard to Jesus. When he persecuted the Christians, he compelled them to affirm the Law's curse on Jesus (Acts 26:11; 1 Cor. 12:3), because for the Jews, a crucified Messiah was a tremendous offense. It went against their preconceptions of the Messiah's work and worthiness. But did the offense lay only there? Hardly. Paul proclaimed that not only had the Messiah been crucified but *God's own Wisdom,* in Jesus, had partaken of suffering, death, and resurrection from the dead. To discuss how the Jews would react to that [preposterous claim], we begin with a parallel theme.

Christology and Monotheism

Practically all historical theology textbooks report that a problem soon arose in the church's Christology as to how faith in a divine Jesus, the Son of God, could be maintained while at the same time holding to Jewish and Old Testament monotheism to which the church was also committed. The traditional view sounds insightful and correct—until one begins to search in the early Christian source material for confirmation that there was a "problem." My opinion is that one cannot find even a trace of such in the sources. Nowhere in the New Testament is monotheism an obstacle to confessing Christ as God—not in the prologue of John (John 1:1–18, where we would expect to find it), nor in 1 Cor. 8:6 (where Paul states with great emphasis that we believe in one God, the Father, and in one Lord, Jesus Christ). It is as though Paul was not aware that, in spite of emphasizing the unity, he is in fact confessing a double God and Lord, the Father *and* the Son. Isn't Paul actually confessing two Gods and two Lords?

The first Christian authors after the New Testament era, those whom we usually call "apostolic fathers," showed a similar lack of concern about the monotheism issue. Ignatius (A.D. 110) called Christ *God* without the slightest hesitation. He seems completely unaware that this might present a problem vis-a-vis Biblical monotheism. And when the problem of monotheism later comes to the fore in the "Apologists" (ca. A.D. 150–80), it is the relationship between God and idolatry that is discussed, not the relationship between the Father and the Son.

This tells us something important about early Christology's Jewish presuppositions and, on the other hand, about the actual offense for Jews. I spoke to this point in the previous chapter but will do so now more directly. From time immemorial, Jewish monotheism was occupied with zealously guarding two positions. One was the struggle against heathendom's idol worship. The other was the battle against philosophically eliminating the boundary between Creator and creation. In reality Judaism deemed this to be one and the same struggle, as Paul the Jew clearly shows in Rom. 1:21–25. *But Judaism was not a stranger to nor was it anxious about the thought of differentiating between dissimilar attributes of God as though God had an inner structure.* [See the summary statement, p. 75.]

As I said earlier, scholars describe the Jewish understanding of God as "dissimilar hypostases."[2] Regardless of whether this term is suitable or not, one can nevertheless without a doubt maintain that, long before the time of Jesus, Judaism was accustomed to speak about personified (hypostasized) aspects of God serving as "agents" or "acting authorities" for God, both for creation and salvation. These "agents" could be God's wisdom, God's name, God's Spirit, or the Lord's host of angels found in the various accounts of the patriarchs and in the Exodus. Later on the rabbis developed a distinctive concept for God's immanence or dwelling among his people, as well as for his abasement: They spoke of God's *Shekinah* (from the Hebrew verb *to dwell*).[3] We have the remarkable discussions about God's word, His *memra,* in the Targum (the Aramaic translation of the Old Testament), which scholars have found difficult to understand.[4] Philo of Alexandria (ca. A.D. 30–40) spoke about a type of triunity in God which he found illustrated in the account of Abraham's encounter with the three men in Genesis 18. What Abraham saw was God Himself and His two highest powers, namely His creative and royal power.[5] In a similar manner, the rabbis spoke of God's two highest "goals" *(middoth),* His justice and His mercy.[6]

It is therefore not so strange that, in spite of talk about a Son of God and an agent who participated in the creation of the world as well as serving as a soteriological mediator between God and humanity, there seems not to have been any *monotheism problem* for the first Christians. The scandal never lay there. Rather it lay in the transference of such traditional hypostasis concepts to a crucified Messiah-pretender from Nazareth. Perhaps the scandal existed primarily because it pointed to a concrete individual.

Christology's Real Scandal: The Incarnation

Justin Martyr's dialogue with Trypho illustrates the incarnation issue with surprising clarity. Justin set forth in two steps the Scriptural proof for the incarnation. First, he shows that the Old Testament is acquainted with a personage who is called both God and Lord (*Kyrios*—and in addition, Wisdom and Glory and a number of other names) but names that are different from the Father (*Dial.* 56–61, cf. 126–29). Next, Justin wishes to prove that it was this personage who became a human being in the person of Jesus (*Dial.* 63ff). Trypho has no problem with the first step. He appears more co-operative than usual and praises Justin for his faithfulness to Scripture in this regard. But the tone of the discussion becomes quite different when Justin proceeds further and seeks to prove that this "God number two"(*deuteros theos*) became the human being called Jesus. At this point Trypho withdraws his earlier admission and reacts to Justin's argumentation with disbelief and loathing: "You seek to prove an unbelievable and impossible thing that God could be born and become a human being" (*Dial.* 68:1).

Let me say it more pointedly: What was scandalous for Judaism in wisdom Christology was not the implied plurality or structure within the essence of God but, from a Jewish perspective, the over-stepping of the boundary between God and humanity which the incarnation implied.

In that regard, the Jewish reaction was similar to the Greek reaction. Hellenistic culture had little knowledge and still less understanding about Jewish messianism; a crucified messiah was hardly scandalous in His role as Messiah because little baggage accompanied this concept. But a crucified Son of God—*that* was to Greek ears a self-contradiction and an absolute impossibility. (I have previously cited testimony concerning this from Celsus and Tertullian, pp. 17–18).

What I have been driving at is how the Jews and Greeks would have tried to lessen the scandal of the incarnation in order to come to faith in Jesus. Both would have had the tendency to eliminate incarnation theology, but in different ways.

From a Jewish perspective, Jesus' humanity was a given. A Messiah who was not truly human was meaningless. Thus an acceptable Jewish Christology had to be *adoptionist,* i.e., the origin of the Messiah had to be that of a mere human being but who had been chosen, *adopted,* for his messianic task and status. We find such a Christology among the *Ebionites* who were second century Jewish Christians.

On the other hand, a consistent Hellenist found it more natural to view Jesus' humanity as a veneer, that Jesus never was touched by suffering and the cross. He only appeared to suffer, but didn't really, because God could not suffer. From the Greek verb *to seem,* we derive the concept *docetism.* It connotes a Christology which maintains that Jesus' humanity was not real but only an outward disguise.

The church's confession of Christ had to be clarified and defined over against these two positions. Thus, we look at two examples from the Early Church.

The Struggle against Docetism: Ignatius

The Letters of Ignatius were written by the bishop of Antioch on his way to martyrdom in Rome. They are genuine letters (in the sense that they are occasional writings evolving out of a particular situation). They contain little systematic or comprehensive doctrinal content. Rather than any coherent presentation, they offer only fragmentary glimpses of Ignatius' Christology. But the fragments are extensive and pointed enough so that a rather clear picture emerges—at least of Ignatius' own Christology and the docetic Christology he opposed.

> *Ignatius:* bishop of Antioch in Syria, arrested and escorted to Rome through Asia Minor ca. A.D. 110. Along the route to martyrdom, Ignatius wrote letters to five congregations in Asia Minor as well as one to the congregation in Rome and one to Bishop Polycarp.

We first look at an assertion that indicates which concepts Ignatius uses when he speaks about the incarnation.

The most divine prophets lived in conformity with Christ Jesus. For this reason they were persecuted, though inspired by His [Christ's] grace to convince the disobedient that there is but one God who manifested Himself through Jesus Christ His Son, who is His Word [Logos] which proceeded from silence [Greek, *sige*] and in every respect pleased Him who sent Him (*Letter to the Magnesians* 8:2).[7]

Note that Ignatius does not seem to feel any problem at all in simultaneously postulating that the prophets proclaimed one God and that this God has revealed Himself through His Son, the Logos (cf. above regarding the absence of a monotheistic problem in early Christology). The background of this statement concerning the Logos is found in John [1:1–14] and parallels the book of *Wisdom* 18:14–15:

For while gentle silence [*sige*] enveloped all things, and night in its swift course was now half gone, Thy all-powerful Word [*Logos*] leaped from heaven, from the royal throne.[8]

Interestingly, we here have one of the earliest identifications of Wisdom with Logos,[9] showing that Ignatius' logos Christology finds its immediate background in this Jewish text. A more specific statement of this same thought is found in Ignatius' *Letter to the Ephesians* 19:1.

Mary's virginity and her giving birth escaped the notice of the prince of this world, as did the Lord's death—those three secrets crying to be told, but wrought in God's silence.[10]

We get the clearest background to Ignatius' linking of *stillness* (silence) to the Logos' emanation and incarnation when we turn to the Jewish document called *4 Ezra*:

O Lord, You spoke at the beginning of creation and said on the first day, "Let heaven and earth be made," and Your word accomplished the work. And then the Spirit was hovering, and darkness and silence embraced everything (6:38–39).[11]

In other words, Ignatius seems to think consistently in terms of creation categories when he speaks of the incarnation of the Logos. As does Wisdom, so the Logos steps forward out of the stillness from which God's creative activity arises. For Ignatius, the creative events surrounded by the same "creative silence" which ruled creation's first day include Jesus' conception, birth, and death. Stated differently, Ignatius' logos Christology has clear rootage in Wisdom. (Cf. his letter to *Ephesians 3:2,* where Ignatius speaks of the Son as the Father's *gnome,* i.e., His thought or will or intention.) At the same time when he writes about the reality of the incarnation, Ignatius turns to messianic Christology. Based on Old Testament prooftexts concerning Jesus' messianic work,[12] Ignatius'account of the events in Jesus' life already has a creedal tone and must be considered intended for that purpose (cf. the expression "in accordance with the Scriptures" found in Paul's 1 Cor. 15:3–8!):

> Be deaf, then, when anyone speaks to you apart from Jesus Christ, who was of the family of David, who was of Mary, who was *truly* born, ate and drank, was *truly* persecuted under Pontius Pilate, was *truly* crucified and died. . . . He was also *truly* raised from the dead when His Father raised Him up *(Letter to the Trallians* 9:1–2).[13]

While the reality of the incarnation is highlighted in most cases by the word *truly (alethos),* Jesus' messianic Davidic Sonship is itself so powerfully underscored by His true humanity that any further emphasis through the use of the word *truly* was considered unnecessary.[14] Ignatius leaves no doubt toward whom the *truly* is directed.

> But if, as some godless men—that is, unbelievers—say, His suffering was only a sham [Greek, *to dokein*], (it is they who are in reality a sham), why am I carrying chains? (Cf. *Trall.* 10:1).

On the basis of this text, we call the opponents of Ignatius *docetists.* He does not give us a direct explanation as to how they defended their position that Jesus only seemed to suffer and die, but all similar sources[15] point in the direction of the ancient dogma of the immutability of God[16] and a general devaluation of the corporeal. Perhaps Ignatius gives us a peephole into the background of his opponents' stance on the immutability of God when he says,

> There is one Physician:
> both flesh and spirit,
> begotten and unbegotten,
> in man, God,

in death, true life,
both from Mary and from God,
first passible and then impassible,[17]
Jesus Christ our Lord (Ignatius, *Letter to the Ephesians* 7:2).

No doubt this dogma concerning God's immutability had stalked Ignatius himself as well as his opponents because he seems to be aware of the great offense his words carry. He is obviously aware of what he is doing when he lists as paradoxes seemingly irreconcilable contradictions: material/spiritual; born/unborn; humanity/God; dead/alive; from Mary/from God; suffering/immune to suffering. Ignatius does not make any attempt to mitigate or solve the paradox. It seems rather that he has an intense affinity for this mode of thinking. His Lord had endured a real cross, and he too was to meet his death in a similar manner. He is fond of expressions like "the passion of Jesus Christ" (Salutation in *Trallians*); "his passion blessed by God" (*Smyrnaeans* 1:2); the congregation in Philadelphia "rejoicing in the passion of our Lord" (Salutation in *Philadelphians*); Ignatius' admonition to the congregation in Rome to allow him to be "an imitator of the passion of my God" (*Romans* 6:3). Ignatius can even speak about the Ephesus congregation receiving new life through "the blood of God" (*Eph.* 1:1).

So we see, Ignatius closely connects his Christology and his openness to martyrdom. This important aspect of his Christology (as well as his doctrine of salvation) tells us something important about the context in which the church's Christology developed. Before we resume this subject, we need to compare Ignatius with the anonymous author who highlights Christology in a different direction: against Judaism (in *The Letter of Barnabas*, ca. A.D. 130).

The Struggle against Jewish Messianism: Barnabas

The Letter of Barnabas was probably written two decades after the letters of Ignatius. It reflects a situation in which church and synagog exist side by side amid great uncertainty as to how Christians should relate to Jews and their law. The main theme is therefore related to questions about the people of God, the covenant, and observance of the law. The author seeks to give the discussion of these questions a Christological mooring (chaps. 5f) and constantly applies Christological themes to his allegorical/typological exegesis of the laws of sacrifice and cleansing (8f; 11f).

The Letter of Barnabas: Attributed to Barnabas in the manuscript but written by an anonymous author ca. A.D. 130. This short monograph describes how Christians should relate to Judaism and how they ought to think about the Old Testament.

The Biblical basis for the Christological in Barnabas is oriented around two poles: (1) Christ's participation in creation; and (2) His suffering, death, resurrection, and return to judge. We look first at the declaration of Christ's creative activity:

> If the Lord submitted to suffer for our souls—He who is Lord of the whole world, to whom God said at the foundation of the world, "Let Us make man in accord with Our image and likeness" —then how is it that He submitted to suffer at the hand of men? (5:5;[18] cf. the somewhat parallel 6:12).

Later in the letter, the author solves the old question of how to explain the plural in Gen. 1:26 ("let *us* make . . . in *our* image") by making it into a dialog between Father and Son, once again borrowing from Jewish wisdom conceptions. In a corresponding Jewish document, God says:

> When I had completed everything, *My wisdom recommended that I create human beings.*[19]

Barnabas obviously is not interested in statements about Christ's creative activity for their own sake. What interests him is the wide gap between this divine status and Jesus' suffering and death. Note that Barnabas does not focus on creation in general but on Christ's participation in *humanity's* creation, the same humanity that would later crucify Him, but also the same humanity which Christ through His death and resurrection would recreate. The central emphasis in Barnabas' use of Scripture is without a doubt Jesus' suffering and death. Here the passages pile up:

> Jesus' death for our sins predicted: Is. 53:5, 7 (*Barn.* 5:2).
> His death by crucifixion predicted: Ps. 22:21; 119:120; 22:17 (*Barn.* 5:13).

His death at the hands of Jews: Is 50:6–9; 28:16; Ps. 118:22, 24; 22:17; 118:12; 22:19; Is. 3:9–11 (*Barn.* 5:14–6:7).

His suffering and second coming, with their counterpart in the Day of Atonement's two sacrificial animals (chap. 7 with reference to Lev. 16 and Zech. 12:10).

The water for purification in Numbers 19 pointing toward His death and our baptism (Barn. 8).

Moses and Joshua, when they battled against Amalek, as types of Jesus' suffering and victory: Ex. 17 (Barn. 12:2–9).

Christ's reign at God's right hand predicted: Ps. 110:1; Is. 45:1.[20]

To summarize, in His suffering, death, and resurrection, Jesus fulfilled the messianic prophecies. As for Ignatius, so for Barnabas the concrete, historical fulfillment of the messianic prophecies "demand" a complete, human realism in the incarnation. Barnabas states this quite explicitly:

> The prophets ... prophesied concerning Him. And He submitted (as a human being to suffer for the very ones He had created, cf. above), so that He might break the power of Death and demonstrate the resurrection from the dead—thus it was necessary for Him to be manifested in flesh ... *so that He might fulfill the promise to the fathers* (5:6–7).[21]

"The promise to the fathers"—the messianic prophecies—are here understood as the promise about a Messiah who suffers for the sins of humankind and thereby conquers death. Barnabas understands that his picture of Jesus (the polarity between the preexistent agent of creation and the crucified Jesus) does not correspond to the then-current Jewish messianism, which undoubtedly had sharper features than its image one hundred years earlier and which in Barnabas' time was in the process of separating itself from the churchly Christology. Barnabas seems to be polemicizing already against the position which Trypho [later] states is the common Jewish faith: that the Messiah was to be a descendant of David in the sense of being nothing more than an ordinary human being (cf. above p. 24). Thus, it is necessary for Barnabas to stress a sharp distinction here. Perhaps that is the reason he himself avoids using *Christ* as a title. (Only once does he use the traditional double name Jesus Christ—2:6). Explicitly he states,

What does Moses say to *Jesus* [Greek for Joshua] son of [Nun], when he had given this name to Him who was a prophet so that all the people might hearken to Him alone? For the Father [through Moses] is making all things clear concerning His Son *Jesus.* Thus Moses says to *Jesus* [Joshua] son of [Nun], to whom he had given this name when he sent Him to spy out the land: Take a book in your hands and write what the Lord says, that *Jesus* the Son of God will cut off the entire house of Amalek by its roots at the end of days. Again notice *Jesus —not the son of a man but the Son of God*, and manifested in flesh by a type. Since, then, they are going to say that Messiah [Christ] is David's Son, David himself—fearing and perceiving the error of the sinners— prophesies, The Lord said to my Lord. . . . (Ps. 110:1). And again, Isaiah says as follows: The Lord says to my Messiah [Christ], the Lord, whose right hand I held . . . [Is. 45:1]. Notice how David says He is *Lord,* and does not say *Son.* (12:8–11).[22]

Barnabas no doubt understood the word about cutting off the house of Amalek in the same way as Justin did twenty years later. *Amalek* represents the demonic powers that Jesus conquered through His death and resurrection.[23] Barnabas implies that this work is beyond human capability and possible only through the power that belongs to God's Son as an agent of creation.

To summarize, in Ignatius and Barnabas we see early Christology defined in two respects. Ignatius emphasizes that God's Logos actually became a human being who suffered and died in the person of Jesus, contrasted with a Hellenistic-docetic Christology that mythologized the incarnation by recourse to an apparition maneuver. Barnabas also stresses the paradoxical reality of the incarnation. The agent of creation allowed Himself to be killed by His own creation. Over against the Jews, Barnabas insists that this was indeed a divine work that a mere human messiah would have been unable to accomplish.

In both Ignatius and Barnabas we see that Wisdom is the category used to describe the relationship between the Father and the preexistent Son. But this is a given and not a problem for either author because neither makes it the subject for further reflection or polemic of any kind. Christology just does not cause a problem with monotheism. But the incarnation raises a problem not only with the

Greek concept of divinity but also with the growing "normative" Jewish messianism.

The Other "Apostolic Fathers"

Having established a closer acquaintance with Ignatius and Barnabas, we move to the *apologists* from the latter half of the second century. Here the sources become much more plentiful.

But in order not to skip over completely the other pertinent literature prior to the apologists, I will add some cursory remarks regarding Christology in connection with some of the remaining *apostolic fathers.*

The Apostolic Fathers:[24]

1 Clement (ca. A.D. 96): A letter from the congregation in Rome to the congregation in Corinth in which the Roman congregation strongly opposes a schism that has developed in the latter. The letter's main theme is the good order and harmony that characterizes the people of God.

The Teaching of the Twelve Apostles (Didache) (ca. A.D. 100): A catechism and manual for baptism, eucharist, prayer, spiritual gifts and ordination.

The Letters of Ignatius (see above)

The Letter of Barnabas (see above)

2 Clement (A.D. 100–140): A sermon written to encourage the maintenance of the grace of baptism in the ethical life. It attacks the Gnostic rejection of the resurrection of the body.

Hermas (ca. A.D. 140–45): A book of admonition in the form of visions and parables. It maintains the possibility of only one amendment of life before the Lord comes.

Most historical theology textbooks give the impression that there were many different Christologies, e.g., a Davidic Christology in *The Teaching of the Twelve Apostles*; a Spirit Christology in *2 Clement* and parts of *Hermas*; and an angel Christology in the other sections of *Hermas*.[25]

That position may not be wrong, but my impression is that the diversities and differences easily can be overstated. As the reader can by now anticipate, I will hold that the concept of Wisdom is the underlying common Christological model found in most of these authors. When *2 Clement* states that before His earthly life Christ was *spirit* (9:5), I maintain that it can easily be understood as referring to a variant of wisdom Christology. For example, Wisdom is identified with God's spirit already in the *Wisdom of Solomon*. And as we shall see below, Christian theologians also felt that Wisdom and Spirit were closely identified, so that, for example, Irenaeus ascribes several of the Wisdom texts to the Spirit, not to the Son. Nor should one forget the close affinity in theological perspective between *1* and *2 Clement*. One cannot help but notice the passage in *1 Clement* that deals with the relationship of Christ to the Father:

> Through Him we fix our eyes on the heights of heaven,
> Through Him we see mirrored[26] the flawless and sublime
>   countenance of God,
> Through Him the eyes of our heart have been opened,
> Through Him our foolish and darkened understanding
>   springs up to the light,
> Through Him the Master has willed that we should taste im-
>   mortal knowledge;
> ... "Since He is the express image of His greatness"....
>   (36:2).[27]

This is wisdom terminology from beginning to end.[28] In spite of the fact that the Christology in *Hermas* is undeniably diverse and to some extent completely baffling, it is interesting to note that we also encounter a spirit Christology not unlike that found in *2 Clement*—and with clear wisdom characteristics[29] as well as an explicit wisdom Christology in its most Jewish form, namely, an explicit identification of Christ and Law.[30]

Finally the eucharistic prayers in *The Teaching of the Twelve Apostles* also include a wisdom Christology. (These prayers have a close parallel in the Jewish wisdom literature that deals with the mealtime of Wisdom.[31])

These scattered remarks here are intended to build a bridge to my next main section: the incarnation theology of the apologists, putting the main emphasis on an investigation of Justin Martyr.

The Christology of the Apologists: Justin

As an introduction, recall that Justin's Scriptural proof for his Christology uses two different traditions. One is dominant in his *First Apology* (ca. A.D. 150), where we meet it in a rather "pure" form. Justin restates Scripture passages and exegesis from earlier Christian sources, but rearranges parts of the material, and interpolates with commentary of various sorts. In the *Dialogue with Trypho,* written about ten years later, Justin returns to these sources but in a much more revised version and combines them with a new primary source in which the shape of Christology is somewhat different. The Christological prooftext traditon we meet in the *Apology* can be characterized as a messianic Christology, while the new Christological tradition Justin introduces in the *Dialogue* can be said to belong to the wisdom type.[32]

Justin Martyr: Born and raised in Neapolis (now Nablus) near Shechem in Samaria; no doubt the son of a Roman official. Was a Platonist who was converted to Christianity as an adult. Lived the last part of his life in Rome, where he wrote his two major extant works:

The Apology: A work in defense of Christians, written ca. A.D. 150. The latter half of this work contains a detailed presentation of Jesus as the Messiah promised in the Old Testament.

Dialogue with Trypho (ca. A.D. 160): A recapitulation of a conversation which no doubt took place. Trypho, a Jew, discusses with Justin whether Jesus is the Messiah and the continuing obligation of the Law. Justin was turned over to the authorities and killed with some of his friends about A.D. 165 because of his outspoken Christian faith.

We look first at the Christological Scriptural evidence in the *Apology.* Justin outlines the evidence broadly in *1 Apology* 31:7:

> In these books of the prophets we found Jesus our Christ foretold as
> • coming,
> • born of a virgin, growing up to man's estate,

- and healing every disease and every sickness, and raising the dead,
- and being hated, and unrecognized, and crucified,
- and dying, and rising again, and ascending into heaven, and being called the Son of God.
- We find it also predicted that certain persons should be sent by Him into every nation to publish these things, and
- that rather among the Gentiles (than among the Jews) men should believe on Him.[33]

The first point I wish to make is that this passage looks indeed like a confession of faith.[34] Let me illustrate this by placing two other texts alongside of Justin's, one which is earlier and one which is later. In Clement of Alexandria (ca. A.D. 200) some fragments of an earlier writing entitled *The Preaching of Peter* (ca. A.D. 125) are preserved. There we read among other things the following:

> But we, unrolling the books of the prophets which we possess, who name Jesus Christ, partly in parables, partly in enigmas, but also unmistakably and in so many words, found
> - His coming and
> - death, and cross . . . and
> - His resurrection and assumption to heaven . . . .
>
> *As it is written,* these things are all that He behoves to suffer, and what should be after Him.[35]

The Old Roman Symbol is extant in both Greek and Latin. The Greek is the original, indicating that the confession evolved in the Roman congregation, perhaps early in the third century, before the congregation in Rome began to use the Latin language in worship. Most of the baptismal confessions in the Western church are developments or modifications of this confession, including the so-called *Apostles' Creed,* which since the time of Charlemagne has been in general use in the Roman Church and since the Reformation in most Protestant communions. The Old Roman Symbol states:

I believe in God the Father Almighty
and in Christ Jesus His only Son our Lord
who was born of the Holy Spirit and the virgin Mary,
was crucified under Pontius Pilate,

> was buried,
> rose up from the dead on the third day,
> ascended into heaven and sits at the right hand of the Father
> from which He will come to judge the living and the dead,
> and in the Holy Spirit,
> the holy church,
> the forgiveness of sins,
> the resurrection of the flesh.

In my opinion, we perceive here a clear tendency toward that type of confession which we later meet in the *Old Roman Symbol*. (See below p. 76) That such a creedal statement is in the process of evolving we see still more clearly a decade after Justin in the writings of Irenaeus (ca. A.D. 190).

> *Irenaeus,* originally from Asia Minor, had seen Polycarp, a disciple of John, during his childhood. He became bishop of Lyons in southern Gaul in A.D. 177 after it had endured severe persecution. In many ways his is a continuation of Justin Martyr's theology.
>
> Extant works:
>
> *Demonstration of the Apostolic Teaching* (ca. A.D. 190), a concise summary of church doctrine.
>
> *A Refutation and Subversion of Knowledge Falsely So-Called* (Gnosis) (ca. A.D. 185–90). Often simply referred to as "Against Heresies" (*Adversus Haereses*).

In Irenaeus we find the following well-known summary of the church's faith:

> The Church . . . has received from the apostles and their disciples this faith:
> [She believes] in one God the Father Almighty, Maker of heaven, and earth, and the sea, and all things that are in them;
> and in one Christ Jesus, the Son of God, who became incarnate for our salvation;
> and in the Holy Spirit, *who proclaimed through the prophets*

the dispensations of God, and the advents (tas oikonomias kai tas elevseis),
- and the birth from a virgin,
- and the passion,
- and the resurrection from the dead,
- and the ascension into heaven . . .
- and His [future] manifestation from heaven (*Adv. Haer.* 1.10.1).[36]

The account of Jesus' life and work in later creedal statements is found in the Second Article, while here it is found in the Third Article, as an account of what *the Spirit* foretold through the prophets. This connection between an accounting of Jesus' life and a reference to everything that had been foretold through the prophets is a common characteristic traceable from 1 Cor. 15, through *The Preaching of Peter*, Justin, and Irenaeus. One point can be nailed down. Clearly, it is *as Messiah* that Jesus in this manner fulfills the prophecy of Scripture. It is hardly an accident that He is called *Christ Jesus,* and not *Jesus Christ* in both Irenaeus and the Old Roman Symbol, because in this forward position *Christ* retains its significance as the title: *Messiah.*[37]

One more common characteristic in this type of Christ-confession is that the writers never begin by speaking about a preexistent Christ. They always begin with Christ's historical advent and virgin birth. In my opinion, the simple reason is that this type of confession seeks to portray Jesus as the one who fulfilled the messianic prophecies starting with His advent and birth. It is His *appearance in history* which is of interest; His preexistence does not belong to a prophecy/fulfillment schema. In Justin's outline, a discussion of preexistence is also lacking. In his enumeration of Scriptural evidence in the Apology, Justin remains faithful to the tradition from which he draws, even though in the *Dialogue with Trypho* one can see how important preexistence concepts were for Justin.[38]

The messianic outline in Justin's Scriptural evidence is revealed through other methods as well. One can, for example, look more closely at the Old Testament texts upon which this evidence rests. What contours can be seen from the Scripture selections? It might be useful to compare Justin's selection with a list of those messianic texts most often cited from the main body of Jewish literature. This list would include the following:[39]

> Gen. 49:10f: Judah will not lose its royal power before the advent of the Messiah.
> Num. 24:17: A *star* (Messiah) shall rise up out of Jacob.
> Is. 11:1–4: The Messiah shall be a descendent of David, endowed by the Spirit of God.
> Micah 5:1–4: The Messiah will be a native of the city of David, Bethlehem.
> Zech. 9:9: He will ride upon a donkey.
> Ps. 2:1–8: God will triumph over His enemies.
> Ps. 72:5,17: His kingdom will be worldwide.

With the possible exception of Zech. 9:9, the strong, triumphant Messiah whom we meet in these texts is completely unambiguous; yet none of these citations are central in the oldest Scriptural evidence for the cross and the resurrection.[40] Rather the opposite is true: The "obvious" texts (Is. 53; Ps. 22; Ps. 69; Ps. 16; Ps. 110:1; Hos. 6:2) do not seem to have played any role in the traditional Jewish messianic expectations. The Messiah's death and resurrection for the sins of the people was an unexpected addition to the traditional Jewish Scriptural evidence for the Messiah.[41] But if the first generation of Christians was interested in proclaming Jesus as Messiah for their Jewish compatriots—Israel's Messiah as foretold by the prophets—one would expect the Christological Scriptural evidence gradually to be expanded so as to encompass the more traditional Jewish material. That, I contend, is exactly what we find. Let us place Justin's Scriptural evidence for Jesus as Messiah next to the Jewish prooftexts. Justin's list includes the following:[42]

> Advent of the Messiah: Gen. 49:10f; Num. 24:17;
> Is. 11:1; 51:5; Ps. 72:17
> Birth of the Messiah: Is. 7:14; Micah 5:1ff
> Concealed adolescence of the Messiah: Is. 9:6a
> Messianic anointing: Is. 11:2f
> Suffering and death: Zech. 9:9; Ps. 22; Is. 53
> Exaltation: Ps. 24:7f
> He sits at the Father's right hand: Ps. 110:1
> Second Advent: Dan. 7:13; Zech. 12:10–12

This Scriptural evidence has a strikingly Jewish contour and, in my opinion, is strengthened if one digs deeper.[43]

For a simple reason I have stressed the affinity of the Jewish-messianic tradition with Justin's Christological tradition: Although it is possible to assume that the church's Christology was moving away from its Jewish starting point, the source materials do not support such a hypothesis. Rather the opposite is true. The outlines of Justin's Scriptural evidence for Jesus' messiahship are in a way more Jewish (i.e., more rabbinic) than we find in the New Testament—for example, in the mission sermons found in the Book of Acts.

As already mentioned, I contend that this pronounced messianic prooftext tradition lies behind the Second Article in the Old Roman Symbol. If a catechumen who had this confession as the required course of study were asked to explain the Scriptural foundation for a Christ-confession, I believe that person would respond *solely* with Old Testament Scriptural evidence for all the stages of Jesus' life, from His birth by a virgin to His return on Judgment Day.

The source for such a position is not only Justin's First Apology. We encounter it still more clearly in the catechetical-pedagogical tradition in Irenaeus' work entitled *The Demonstration of the Apostolic Preaching*.[44] Here also a structured Christ-confession is presented with the Scriptural undergirding completely drawn from the Old Testament. More than that, we come upon elements of Jewish tradition in both the Old Testament textual transmission and the interpretation rendered by Irenaeus.[45] So it seems that Christian interpretation remained open to contact and influence from Jewish sources.

It would have been futile, Pinchas Lapide maintains, if Paul (or some other Christian missionary) in Corinth or Rome had proclaimed the Son of David to be the anointed *Jewish Messiah*. "They would not know what he was talking about."[46] Perhaps, but that was exactly what Paul and Justin and Irenaeus did, prompted by (one could answer) their common faith in the Old Testament as holy Scripture.

But they also found the other type of Christology, wisdom Christology, in the Old Testament. Why did they not allow it to become dominant? I think the reason may have something to do with the challenge from Marcion and the Gnostics.

Marcion: A native of Sinope, located on the south shore of the Black Sea in Asia Minor. Was exposed there as a heretic by Polycarp. Came to Rome ca. A.D. 140 but was excommunicated as a heretic after a few years. In the book *Antitheses,* Marcion seeks to point out many contradictions between the Old Testament's portrayal of God and the "Father in heaven" from which Jesus proceeded and about whom He preached. The God of the Old Testament, Marcion believes, is not identical with the Father of Jesus Christ but is a hateful and lesser deity who is responsible for the creation of the world. Marcion accepts the Old Testament as literally true in a historical sense but dismisses its god as spiteful and inferior. The same applies to the messianic prophecies. They are to be understood as the Jews understood them. They announce a national warrior king, and the Jews are correct in believing that such a Messiah has yet to come! Marcion also defends a "cleansed" New Testament in which are cut away the accounts of Jesus' birth, citations from the Old Testament, and other matters that would indicate that Jesus (or Paul) acknowledge the God of the Old Testament.

Gnosticism: The common name for a series of doctrinal systems that developed in the second century A.D. Some groups announced themselves as the genuine version of Christianity. The following basic views are common to most Gnostics: Humanity is a stranger in this world because our existence comes from a completely different world: the divine. Originally, peace and harmony reigned in the divine world. God was in everything, and everything was held together by God through the different powers within Him. God was fullness (Greek, *pleroma*). But an inexplicable fall occurred among the powers, which found themselves on the outer edge of this fullness. Some of the divine essence confusedly separated itself from the fullness, and in its confusion this separated part of God created the material world. In this material world, the confused divine essence has become a prisoner and can be found in the divine spark within

> the human soul or spirit. But the problem with the divine spark is that it lives in ignorance. It has forgotten its divine origin. Salvation therefore consists in the human soul receiving the necessary *knowledge* (Greek, *gnosis*), knowledge from whence it came and how it might return thither. The Gnostic systems that acknowledge Jesus view Him therefore as a transmitter of salvific *knowledge*. Christ is a *teacher*.

Marcion, an independent and original theologian, exercised great influence on the congregation in Rome A.D. 140–50. The Gnostics represented a myriad of smaller groups with divergent theological systems. Common to both the Gnostics and Marcion was a radical rejection of the whole work of creation together with the God of creation, the God of the Old Testament. But Marcion and the Gnostics adopted quite dissimilar positions vis-a-vis the Old Testament.

Marcion insisted that the Old Testament be understood literally in its historical sense and that the Jewish interpretation was correct—an unfortunate reality for both the Old Testament and the Jews, contended Marcion, who had nothing but revulsion for the God he met in the Old Testament. Yet he found himself in a paradoxical alliance with the Jews regarding the interpretation of the Old Testament; he insisted that the Jews were correct in contending that Jesus did not correspond to the messianic prophecies of Scripture. One could count on the God of the Old Testament some day sending such a Messiah;[47] but Jesus had nothing to do with the Old Testament, its God, or the messianic prophecies.

The position of the Gnostics differed from Marcion[48] in that they acknowledged parts of Scripture, especially the first chapter of Genesis, as having significant authority and made this chapter the subject of a detailed allegorical/mythological interpretation. Many Gnostics maintained that there was a parallel between the Fall and restoration. While they had considerable insight into the account of creation (which they obviously interpreted as an account of a fall or accident), they had little understanding about Old Testament messianism. They no doubt instinctively felt themselves outside God's *yes* toward the created world that lay built into messianism. In any case, Gnostic literature can be characterized by a virtual aloofness toward Old Testament messianic prophecies and its corresponding messianic

Christology. They did not adopt a polemical stance as Marcion, nor did they object to a figurative interpretation; they just did not deal with the subject.

Confronted with this double challenge by Marcion and the Gnostics, the second century church was pushed to a new consciousness regarding its Jewish roots and its Old Testament legacy. The church not only had to strengthen its reliance upon the Old Testament; but, because Marcion had agreed with the Jews that Jesus was not the Messiah of the Old Testament, the church had to defend the traditional messianic Scriptural evidence and expand upon it against the Gnostics as well as Marcion. It was no theoretical situation in the second century when one who was about to be baptized confessed Jesus as the Messiah whom the Father had promised His people in the Old Testament. I believe we here have important background for understanding why the Second Article in the Old Roman Symbol is so decidedly messianic.

I obviously have to admit that this messianic Christology with its distinctive "Jewish" prophetic evidence was not the only Christology with which these early church fathers were acquainted. Recall the many instances when Justin, in the *Dialogue with Trypho*, alludes to another Christological tradition, the wisdom type: Christ is identified with the Wisdom that speaks in Prov. 8:22ff (*Dial.* 61); among the designations that Scripture uses for Christ is Wisdom (*Dial.* 61:1; 62:4); the Father speaks to the Son about creating the human race in Gen. 1:26ff (*Dial.* 62:1).

While Jewish interpreters viewed Wisdom as God's active agent in those instances when *God* is said to appear on earth (*Wisdom* 10ff), Justin introduces the point of view that it was the *Son* who appeared in all those instances where Scripture speaks of God appearing on earth (*Dial.* 56–60; 126:6; 127:1, 3f). In a detailed presentation, Justin emphasizes that the "angel of the Lord" who appears in various places in the stories about Abraham, Jacob and Moses is not identical with God the Father, yet on the other hand, is said to be "Lord" and "God." *This Wisdom and Logos of God is what became human in Jesus!* We are confronted with the same two-pronged Christ-confession that we met in Barnabas. Justin knows how to express this in beautiful fashion as seen in the following passage:

> We find recorded in the memoirs of His apostles that He is

the Son of God; and since we call Him the Son, we have understood that He proceeded before all creatures from the Father by
His power and will (for He is addressed in the writings of the
prophets in one way or another as Wisdom, and the Day, and the
East. . . .); and that He became man by the Virgin in order that the
disobedience which proceeded from the serpent might receive
its destruction in the same manner in which it derived its origin.
For Eve, who was a virgin and undefiled, having conceived the
word of the serpent, brought forth disobedience and death. But
the Virgin Mary received faith and joy, when the angel Gabriel
announced the good tidings to her that the Spirit of the Lord would
come upon her, and the power of the Highest would overshadow
her: wherefore also the Holy Thing begotten of her is the Son of
God; and she replied, "Be it unto me according to thy word." And
by her has He been born, to whom we have proved so many
Scriptures refer, and by whom God destroys both the serpent and
those angels and men who are like Him; but works deliverance
from death to those who repent of their wickedness and believe
upon Him (*Dial.* 100:4–6).[49]

The many passages in Justin like this may be summarized as
follows: Christ is the true Son of God, the second Adam, who re-
verses the fall and damage caused by the first Adam. He defeats the
devil who at one time had overcome Adam. He had to become a
human being in order to accomplish the work of re-creation through
His suffering, death and resurrection. He who acted as the effective
agent during the first creation came in a double sense to His own
when He came to earth. *This is the Christ-confession that holds creation and salvation together.* It confesses Christ as the Lord of creation and history; Christ is a concrete reality in the whole of Old
Testament history, not just a heralding Messiah. He is *the active and
speaking subject* in the important events in the history of the
people.[50]

Thus, Justin's confession constructs a bridge between creation
and redemption. The declaration of Christ's creative activity pre-
pares for declarations concerning Christ's salvific work. Listen to
Justin's own condensed statement of this Christology directed
against Marcion and quoted by Irenaeus:

I would not have believed the Lord [Christ] Himself, if He had
announced any other than He who is our framer, maker, and

nourisher. But because the only-begotten Son came to us from the one God, who both made this world and formed us, and contains and administers all things, summing up His own handiwork in Himself,[51] my faith towards Him is steadfast, and my love to the Father immoveable, God bestowing both upon us.[52]

Just as Justin uses the connection between creation and redemption in his polemic against Marcion, so Irenaeus later does the same on the much broader front against the Gnostics.

But Justin uses wisdom Christology in another way: to counter Greek philosophy. I mentioned earlier that a fundamental characteristic of the Jewish concept of Wisdom (as we meet it in the *Wisdom of Solomon*) is the struggle against the worship of idols, the very definition of foolishness. Idolatry connotes a lack of Wisdom, while true fear of God is the presupposition of Wisdom, yes, its very expression. By stating the concept of Wisdom in such a decidedly Jewish manner (the struggle between God and idols), Jewish teachers who focused on Wisdom [and thus might be thought of as having "Hellenizing" tendencies] reveal how deeply Jewish they were in their thinking.

But Justin also thought in this frame of reference.[53] For him, humanity's great need and misfortune is its bondage to idolatry, in reality to demons who have deluded human beings into worshipping them as gods. Thus, Justin stands in the same tradition as two Jewish writings from the intertestamental period, *The Book of Jubilees* and *The First Book of Enoch*; and, as the first Christian author, Justin repeats the *Book of Enoch's* explanation as to the origin of idolatry:

> God, when He had made the whole world, and subjected things earthly to man, and arranged the heavenly elements for the increase of fruits and rotation of the seasons, and appointed this divine law . . . committed the care of men and of all things under heaven to angels whom He appointed over them. But the angels transgressed this appointment, and were captivated by love of women, and begat children who are called demons; and besides, they afterwards subdued the human race to themselves, partly by magical writings, and partly by fears and punishments they occasioned, and partly by teaching them to offer sacrifices, incense, and libations, of which things they stood in need after they were enslaved by lustful passions; and among men they sowed murders,

wars, adulteries, intemperate deeds, and all wickedness. Whence also the poets and mythologists, not knowing that it was the angels and those demons who had been begotten by them that did these things to men, and women, and cities, and nations, which they related, ascribed them to God Himself (*2 Apol.* 5:2–5).[54]

In such a context, Justin believes, some of the philosophers (namely those who have rejected Homer's gods as demons) have a share in the truth, Logos and Wisdom—especially Socrates. Justin approves of Socrates' sharp critique leveled at the Homeric gods (as Plato reports in *The Republic*), which Justin combined with the accusation made against Socrates during his trial. Justin's view is that Socrates became a martyr for the same reason that Christians became martyrs: they refused to worship the gods of the Athenians. So, in the eyes of Justin, Socrates is truly a "wise" man:

> When Socrates endeavored, by true reason and examination, to bring these things to light and deliver men from the demons, then the demons themselves, by means of men who rejoiced in iniquity, compassed [brought about] his death, as an atheist and a profane person, on the charge that "he was introducing new divinities"; and in our case they display similar activity. For not only among the Greeks did reason (Logos) prevail to condemn these things through Socrates, but also among the Barbarians they were condemned by Reason (or the Word, the Logos) Himself, who took shape, and became man, and was called Jesus Christ; and in obedience to Him, we not only deny that they who did such things as these are gods, but assert that they are wicked and impious demons (*1 Apol.* 5:3–4).[55]

Some rabbis say that a non-Jew who rejects idolatry and turns his back on it can be considered a Jew even if he isn't one and that he can be reckoned as having kept the whole Law.[56] (In the rabbinic legends, especially Abraham and the three young men in the fiery furnace—Shadrach, Meshach and Abednego as in Dan. 3—are proto-examples of those who reject idolatry and hold to the one God, even under threat of losing their lives. Abraham was also thrown into a "furnace" when he broke with his father's idol worship.)[57]

In a similar manner, Justin considers Socrates to be a "Christian" and for the same reason. One can see just how close Justin is to the Jewish tradition from the following passage:

> Lest some, without reason, maintain that we say that Christ was born one hundred and fifty years ago ... and should cry out against us as though all men who were born before Him were irresponsible, let us anticipate and solve the difficulty. We have been taught that Christ is the first-born of God, and we have declared above that He is the Word of whom every race of men were partakers; and those who lived reasonably are Christians, even though they have been considered atheists; as, among the Greeks, Socrates and Heraclitus, and men like them; and among barbarians, Abraham, Ananias, Azarias and Mishael .... (*1 Apol.* 46:1–3).[58]

Just as the rabbis could consider unbelievers who broke with idolatry as a kind of honorary Jew, so for the same reasons Justin counted some of the philosophers as Christians. (His typical rabbinic grouping of the four men in the furnace reveals how Jewish-oriented his thoughts were.)[59]

In this context Justin speaks of Christ as the *Logos spermatikos,* "the sown Logos," referring to Christ as an agent of creation, who has given us human reason as a weapon against succumbing to idolatry, so that people are without excuse when they allow themselves to be deluded by demons.[60]

When Justin calls Christianity the true philosophy and as a Christian missionary wears the cloak of a philosopher, he is steeped in the most profound Greek understanding of the task of philosophy. The striking thing about Justin is not a Hellenistic definition of Christianity but his loftiest Jewish definition of philosophy!

Justin paints this overall picture of the incarnate Christ: As God's own Wisdom and Logos, Christ was a co-worker in creating the world and the human race. But as a result of idolatry, they came under an alien authority. They became enslaved by demons and made themselves unclean through sacrifices and gross sins. They became fools. Only in isolated cases did a person manage to see through this delusion. But in Christ, the Wisdom and Logos of God became a human being. Through His death and resurrection He broke the power of the demons. In His name, victory is to be found over both sin and the demonic. By becoming a human being (the new Adam), Christ absorbed into Himself the fallen and alienated work of creation and gave humanity access to a new creation.

For Christ, being the first-born of every creature, became again the chief of another race regenerated by Himself through water, and faith, and wood, containing the mystery of the cross; even as Noah was saved by wood when he rode over the waters with his household (*Dial.* 138:2)[61]

The latter is He after whom and by whom the Father will renew both the heaven and the earth (*Dial.* 113:5).[62]

When we look back upon Justin's Christology and ask what offended Greek ears, there can hardly be any doubt about the answer: In spite of all Justin's Jewish way of thinking, it was the incarnation.

And what was offensive to Trypho's Jewish ears? Also the incarnation! Not logos Christology as such; not the idea of a Wisdom/Logos co-working in the creation of the world; but to believe that this Wisdom/Logos had become a human being in the son of a carpenter from Nazareth—that was for Trypho "unbelievable and impossible" (*Dial.* 68:1). This impression can be strikingly illustrated if we turn to one of the apologists who followed Justin.

The Christology of the Apologists: Theophilus

In his three books *To Autolycus*, Theophilus delivers a detailed apology [defense] against heathendom. It is a work that could just as well have been written by a Jew. In these books the incarnation is not even mentioned—implied, but not actually discussed. In the few Christological sections there is hardly anything to which a Jew would have taken exception.

Theophilus: Bishop of Antioch, influenced by Jewish-Christian traditions. From his extensive works, only three books *To Autolycus* (ca. A.D. 180) are extant. Autolycus had publicly attacked Christianity. Theophilus demonstrates that Old Testament monotheism is superior to the worship of idols and that Old Testament revelation is older and more trustworthy than the Greek myths.

In the first place, in complete harmony [the prophets] taught us that He made everything out of the non-existent. . . . Therefore God, having His own Logos innate in His own bowels,[63] generated Him together with His own Sophia [Wisdom], vomiting Him forth before everything else. He used this Logos as His servant in the things created by Him, and through Him He made all things (cf. John 1:3; Col. 1:16). He [Logos] is called Beginning because He leads and dominates everything fashioned through Him (Gen. 1:1). It was He, Spirit of God (Gen. 1:2) and Beginning (Gen. 1:1) and Sophia (Prov. 8:22) and Power of the Most High (Luke 1:35), who came down into the prophets and spoke through them about the creation of the world and all the rest.[64] For the prophets did not exist when the world came into existence; there were the Sophia of God which is in Him and His holy Logos who is always present with Him. For this reason He says through Solomon the prophet, "When He prepared the heaven, I was with Him" (Prov. 8:27–29). And Moses, who lived many years before Solomon—or rather, the Logos of God speaking through him as an instrument—says: "In the Beginning God made heaven and earth." For the divine Sophia knew in advance that some persons were going to speak nonsense and make mention of a multitude of non-existent gods. Therefore, in order for the real God to be known through His works and to show that by His Logos God made heaven and earth and what is in them, He said: "In the Beginning God made heaven and earth" (*To Autol. 2:10*).[65]

As one can clearly see from the conclusion of this passage, Theophilus is blissfully unaware that his logos Christology presents any kind of a problem in relationship to Old Testament monotheism. A Jew, with good reason, also could have said the same. The only thing which reveals that the author is a Christian is the doubling of Wisdom when Theophilus speaks of both the Word [Logos] in Wisdom's role and Wisdom in its original role alongside the Word. A Jewish author would have identified the two as Justin still does. This doubling allows Theophilus also to place the Spirit in the category of Wisdom. In 2:15, Theophilus therefore can speak of "the triad of God and His Logos and His Sophia."[66] The same doubling of Wisdom appears in Theophilus's interpretation of the plural subject found in Gen. 1:26.[67] If we connect this passage to 2:22 where Theophilus explains that, when God wandered in Paradise and spoke with Adam, it was none other than the Word [Logos], the agent of creation, who is God's counselor, mind and thought, and who first was "within" (*endiatheton*) God, but who prior to creation stepped forward as an "outer" word (*touton ton logon egennêsen proforrikon*).[68] These are also the Christological texts in this important book. The rest of the book is a detailed defense of Old Testament monotheism, of the Old Testament prophets' greater age than the Greek "fathers," and for the historical reliability of the Old Testament. The whole is constructed upon earlier Jewish apologetics. A Jew from Antioch would hardly have had any complaint about Theophilus's work; it must therefore be the doubling of Wisdom. But more serious than that, it could hardly have been because the incarnation is not to be found here [in Theophilus's work].

So it does not mean that Theophilus was not an incarnation theologian. It only means that the opposition against which he was protecting himself (Greek polytheism) was directed primarily against Old Testament monotheism and that this was the foremost matter that needed to be defended.[69]

Incarnation and Martyrdom

In closing this chapter, let me touch upon a point that was mentioned in connection with Ignatius (regarding the existential nature of Christology) that must never be forgotten lest one have a warped understanding of Christology as a dogma that the church displays for its intellectual elite. The point to consider is the connection between Christology and martyrdom.

Those who had a docetic Christology derided Ignatius's chains, or so he thought. It is not difficult to find Gnostic documents from the second century that actually made fun of the martyrdom of "ordinary" Christians. In one of the Gnostic documents found at Nag Hammadi in 1945, *The Testimony of Truth*, Christians are criticized for two things: They fulfill the law of the Creator God by marrying and begetting children, and they hasten to martyrdom. Both reveal how hopelessly Christians are addicted to this world and its power, while Gnostics with their inner freedom and superiority cast the created world and all externality behind them. They are therefore not touched by anything that happens to one's body.[70] Not all Gnostics were equally adverse to martyrdom; some sought to understand Jesus' suffering and death as a model for the inner person's strength and victory over the body and its fleshly desires. These Gnostics could also say yes to martyrdom,[71] but that seems to have been the exception rather than the rule. Elaine Pagels is no doubt correct when she says, "One thing is clear: one's position on martyrdom determined how one interpreted Jesus' passion and death."[72] Christians confessed belonging to the Lord at the risk of their lives—that is, those who were at risk were those who followed Him in the old Jewish manner (which Christians from the very first were convinced was the correct way), namely, rejecting every other form of veneration whether it was to the emperor or a Roman god. That was the kind of Lord Christians followed. Irenaeus articulately expresses how impossible it would have been to follow Christ into martyrdom if one had not been convinced that He also, in His passion and death, had gone on before them and that the way He had blazed for them did not end there but led forward to the resurrection, the bodily resurrection from the dead, when the martyr received a brand new body in place of that which the torturers, wild animals, and flames had destroyed.

> This likewise [answers] those who maintain that He suffered only in appearance. For if He did not truly suffer, no thanks to Him, since there was no suffering at all; and when we shall actually begin to suffer, He will seem to be leading us astray, exhorting us to endure buffeting, and to turn the other cheek, if He himself did not in reality suffer the same before we did.... The Son of God is truly good and patient, the Word of God the Father having been made the Son of man. For He fought and conquered ... through obedience doing away with disobedience completely: for He bound the strong man, and set the weak free, and endowed His own handiwork with salvation by destroying sin. For He is a most holy and merciful Lord and loves the human race (*Against Heresies* 3.18.6).[73]

While I agree with Elaine Pagels on the connection between Christology and martyrdom, I disagree with her overall picture of the relationship between Gnostic and Orthodox Christianity and their respective relationship to the New Testament. But on the topic that we now are discussing, I think she has expressed the matter better than most:

> In its portrait of Christ's life and passion, orthodox teaching offered a means of interpreting fundamental elements of human experience. Rejecting the Gnostic view that Jesus was a spiritual being, the orthodox insisted that He, like the rest of humanity,

73

was born, lived in a family, became hungry and tired, ate and drank wine, suffered and died. They even went so far as to insist that He rose *bodily* from the dead. Here again, as we have seen, orthodox tradition implicitly affirms bodily experience as the central fact of human life. What one does physically—one eats and drinks, engages in sexual life or avoids it, saves one's life or gives it up—all are vital elements in one's *religious* development. But those Gnostics who regarded the essential part of every person as the "inner spirit" dismissed such physical experience, pleasurable or painful, as a distraction from spiritual reality—indeed, as an illusion. No wonder, then, that far more people identified with the orthodox portrait than with the "bodiless spirit" of Gnostic tradition. Not only the martyrs, but all Christians who have suffered for 2,000 years, who have feared and faced death, have found their experience validated in the story of the *human* Jesus.[74]

Let me attempt a quick summary of this chapter. We first asked wherein the offense in Christology truly lay from a Jewish perspective. We found that it was not in and of itself offensive to speak about an inner structure in God so that, for example, His Wisdom could be spoken of as an attribute within God. That which was offensive lay in (1) the idea that this side of God, Wisdom, had become a human being of flesh and blood and (2) especially in the account about the death of the Son on a cross. Here lay also the offense for the Greeks. We saw how Ignatius had to struggle against Hellenistic docetism which dilutes the offense of the incarnation by denying the reality of the incarnation. Barnabas has to fight against the opposite in Jewish messianism which denies Jesus' divinity and considers Him only a human messiah.

This did not mean that the second century church abandoned the old confession of Jesus as Messiah. As a result of the challenge from Marcion and the Gnostics, the church was called upon to retain its Jewish roots, especially in its Christology. A decidedly messianic prooftext tradition threaded its way from 1 Cor. 15, through Barnabas, *The Preaching of Peter,* Justin, Irenaeus and into the second article of "the Old Roman Symbol."

Alongside this messianic Christology, we have followed wisdom Christology in both the writings of the apostolic fathers as well as the apologists. We have observed the strong continuity with New Testament Christology have seen how this wisdom Christology

74

could provide an author like Justin Martyr with important tools to meet the challenge of Greek philosophy. In the midst of this encounter, we saw how Jewish was the mindset of an apparently entrenched Hellenistic theologian.

Finally, we looked at the existential side of a Christ-confession. This involved the relationship between the incarnation and the reality of Christ's suffering on the one side and, on the other, Christian martyrdom as a result of confessing Christ.

4

Christology in East and West

Christology and Geography

The many and long quarrels over Christology during the fourth and fifth centuries may at first glance seem difficult to grasp. To come to grips with them, we need a few simple models [or paradigms] to make sense of it all. I think we will come a long way if we take our starting point from an otherwise simple geographic model: a separation between East and West.[1] By East is meant the Eastern half of the Mediterranean, from Greece around in a semicircle to Cyrene (in what today is Libya). By West is meant the Mediterranean lands from Italy around in a semicircle to the lands around Carthage (in what today is Algeria and Tunisia). Then we can distinguish in the model the various theological centers in East and West. In the West are Rome and Carthage; in the East are Alexandria, Antioch, and Ephesus. The five cities just mentioned were for that matter the five largest cities in the Roman Empire during the pre-Constantinian era.

With this brief geographic sketch, I believe it is possible to draw some relatively simple lines in what otherwise is a very complicated picture during the fourth and fifth centuries.

First, note a fundamental difference between East and West: the very central confession of faith—the Trinitarian confession spoken each time a person was baptized. We usually speak of "three articles" in this baptismal confession, and in this chapter we will focus on the second article concerning the Son of God.

The Second Article of the Baptismal Confession: The Old Roman Symbol

Scholars have long accepted the view that all the Western baptismal confessions, including the *Apostles' Creed,* derive from the so-called

Old Roman Symbol, which seems to have become established (first in Greek) in the course of the first decades of the third century.[2] Although the research surrounding the history of baptismal confessions in the Early Church used to say that even the Eastern baptismal confessions were dependent upon the Old Roman Symbol,[3] this position was abandoned largely through the studies of Hans Lietzmann.[4] Today the general consensus is that neither of the primitive forms or archetypes was derived from the other. Each is independent; they stand alongside each other, each with its own unmistakable peculiarities.

Before we go any further, it is useful to read the Western and Eastern baptismal confessions next to each other. For an Eastern confession we have selected the one Eusebius of Caesarea presented to the Council of Nicea in 325. The document deserves special attention. We will return to it later, but for the moment it is interesting just to compare it with the Old Roman Symbol.

The Old Roman Symbol [West]	*The Baptismal Confession in Caesarea [East]*
Second Article	*Second Article*
(I believe) in Christ Jesus, His only Son, our Lord	(I believe) in one Lord Jesus Christ, God's Logos (John 1:1) God from God, light from light, life from life (cf. Wis. 7:26; John 5:26) only begotten Son (John 1:14, 18) the firstborn before every creature (Col. 1:15) born of the Father before all times (Prov. 8:24ff) *through whom all things were created* (John 1:3)
who was born of the Holy Spirit and the virgin Mary	who for our salvation became flesh and dwelt among us human beings (John 1:14)

was crucified under Pontius Pilate, was buried,	suffered,
arose from the dead on the third day	arose on the third day
ascended into heaven and sits at the Father's right hand	ascended to the Father
from whence He will come to judge the living and the dead.	and will come again to judge the living and the dead.

In previous comments about the Old Roman Symbol's second article, I argued that it is a list that provides a prooftext approach for Jesus' messianic work—stated otherwise, prooftexts of a prophetic/fulfillment type. It is His historical appearance from birth to second advent that is the subject for a quick retelling. Therefore the Symbol says nothing explicit about Jesus' preexistence. At first glance, this confession seems to lack a statement on preexistence and incarnation, but J.N.D. Kelly and others have argued conclusively that these are to be found, literally, between the lines. In the introductory line about Christ Jesus our Lord, there is also found the phrase "God's *only* Son" (*monogenēs*). Since this Johannine expression is not used much in the literature before the Old Roman Symbol,[5] scholars have asked why exactly this term came to be used; other terms could have been employed. The answer no doubt is found in Irenaeus, who states that some of the Gnostics made *monogenēs* one of their central concepts. The word connoted a *power* (*aeon*) in heaven which they sharply distinguished from the earthly Jesus. Irenaeus answers at length by arguing that the preexistent, heavenly *monogenēs* is identical with the human Jesus (*Against Heresies* 3.16.1). It is not unreasonable to suppose that the term *monogenēs* was included in the confession for that purpose and meaning: The preexistent *monogenēs* was none other than He who became a human being through Mary! At the same time, because this confession very effectively maintained Jesus' historical reality as the Messiah promised in the Scriptures, it also implicitly spoke of His heavenly lineage.

The Second Article of the Baptismal Confession: The Eastern Confessions

We now compare the Old Roman Symbol [ORS] with the second article of the confession of Eusebius of Caesarea cited above. One can not help but be struck by how radically different the structure and proportions are in this confession compared to the ORS. The story of Jesus' life is told in the shortest possible manner, much shorter than in the ORS. On the other hand, Christ's divine preexistence is detailed, and His work as an agent of creation is singled out. It will be almost too obvious to the reader that here we have wisdom Christology. Christ is portrayed in wisdom categories which (in my opinion) He himself alludes to in various New Testament passages.[6]

Taken as a whole, there are two poles in the structure of Eusebius's second article:

• The preexistent Christ is an agent of creation.
• The incarnate Christ saves His own work of creation through the cross and resurrection.

Preexistence, divine status, and creative activity are clustered around the first pole. Around the other is the incarnation, passion, and resurrection. There is a tremendous drama here, both in the point of Christ's changeover from preexistence to incarnation and in the way that the confession describes it. As the confession explicitly states, everything has occurred "for the sake of our salvation" (an emphasis found in all of the Eastern confessions). While the messianic Christological tradition that evolves into the ORS obviously is thinking along an *historical* time line (prophecy/fulfillment), the Eastern polarity is between divine glory and human debasement, similar to what we found in Ignatius and Barnabas and the wisdom Christology of Justin (all of them Eastern theologians). Not that Easterners were unconversant with prophetic/fulfillment Christology; obviously they were. The two Christological models are found side by side in both Eastern and Western theologians—e.g., Justin and Irenaeus, two Eastern theologians, for whom messianic Christology is central and inexpendable; and Tertullian, a Western theologian who accords wisdom Christology a dominant role. (More about this later). It is not a matter of either/or, but it is clear that East and West place the accent differently in their baptismal confessions.

In the West, we do not know of any disagreement concerning the second article and scarcely any concerning Christology in the strict sense of the word. To be sure, Tertullian strongly opposed any identification of the Father and the Son, but that was more a trinitarian dispute than a Christological one. And during the second century in Rome, some seem to have advocated an outright adoptionist Christology, but they appear to have been a peripheral group, and they caused no large dispute.[7]

All the significant Christological disputes poured themselves out within the Eastern church. While all the essential features of the baptismal confessions seem to have been held in common at the various Eastern theological centers, the parting of the ways took place in the details. The Eastern commonality was its wisdom Christology—in which the offense of the incarnation lay inherently. And it was there in coming to grips with this harsh offense that various solutions were championed.

Christology in the East: Antioch

We have already met a representative of Antiochene theology: Theophilus.[8] Theophilus does not write a single sentence about the incarnation. Yet, from all the hints we find, we can picture his understanding of incarnation theology. Theophilus speaks of a Wisdom or Logos incarnation in the prophets, who "contained in themselves" *(choresantes)* the Wisdom/Logos of God. Could it be that Theophilus would have spoken of Jesus in essentially the same categories, that is, of Jesus inspired by God's preexistent wisdom, so that Wisdom dwelt in the human Jesus in about the same way as in the prophets, only in a larger and more complete manner so as to make Him the best, final, and perfect prophet?

This is speculation. But it is not completely unfounded. A good half century after Theophilus, a very able theologian occupied the bishopric of Antioch who thought exactly like that. He was Paul of Samosata.[9]

Paul of Samosata: Bishop of Antioch from ca. 260. Deposed by a synod in 268 because of heresy and "arrogance." The theologians who deposed him were influenced by

Origen and represented the Alexandrian tradition in Christology.

Paul stressed two matters: It seemed important for him to emphasize that the Father was one, as well as the fact that just because God was said to contain the Logos, that in no way compromised His unity. Before citing a key statement on this point, we must introduce two concepts that we will often encounter and that are unavoidable when discussing Christology: *hypostasis* and *prosopon*.

Hypostasis: A thing or person can be said to have a number of attributes: size, color, weight, etc. These attributes do not exist independently from the thing or person but only *in* it. The thing or person, on the other hand, does not exist *in* something else but exists by itself. The thing contains attributes, is under the control of the attributes, so that together they appear as a thing. That part of the thing or person which is subsumed under the specific attributes and which bears them is called *substantia* in Latin (*sub:* under, *stantia:* that which is permanent), and *hypostasis* in Greek (*hypo:* under, and *stasis:* that which is permanent). The concept, therefore, comes close to the idea of *essence*. It was used most often in Latin (and sometimes in Greek) with just this meaning. But it could also, especially when used of persons, signify those collective attributes by which a thing/person manifests itself as *one* object or individual (approximating "person"). That was how the Greek word *hypostasis* was often used. It comes close in meaning to the second concept:

Prosopon: This word originally meant *face* and can designate an individual person or individual thing in a group. Used with regard to persons, it means an *individual,* i.e., a *personality* or *personal being,* even if normally translated *person.* When, for example, Paul of Samosata in a citation below states that the Father and His Logos are one *prosopon,* he means that the Logos is not an independent individual alongside the Father but that the Logos is an attribute of God. Thus God and His Logos are one individual, one *prosopon.* Stated differently, the Logos is not a *hypostasis* be-

> cause the Logos does not exist by itself but only as an attribute in God.

Paul of Samosata, in a primary assertion, states,

> God is a single person with the Word [Logos] just as a man and his word are one (Pollard, 114).

We are confronted here with a Christian theologian for whom Christology, as it relates to the unity of God, has become a problem.[10] Paul of Samosata solved this problem by viewing God's Wisdom or Logos (the terms seem to have been synonymous for him) as an impersonal power within God which normally is "introverted" in God and only emanates as a separate quantity when God speaks (sends out His word). But the Word has neither its own *prosopon* nor *hypostasis* alongside of God.

The other anchor in Paul of Samosata's theology is his understanding of the incarnation.

> The Word was not a man; He dwelt in a man[11]—in Abraham, in Moses, in David, in the prophets, and finally in Christ "as in a temple." As in each of the prophets, so also is the dwelling of the divine Word in Him. Consequently, there are in Christ two natures separated from each other and without anything in common with each other; Christ Himself is one thing, and the divine Word which dwells in Him is another.[12]
>
> The Word was greater than Christ, for Christ became great through Wisdom; let us not lower the dignity of Wisdom. For the Word is from above: Jesus Christ the man is from below. Mary has not given birth to the Word, for she did not exist before all ages. Mary has received the Word, and she is not older than the Word; but she has given birth to a man like us, although better in all things, since the grace which came upon Him is from the Holy Spirit, from the promises, from the Scriptures. Thus the anointed Son of David is not alien to Wisdom, and Wisdom does not dwell in this manner in any other; for it was in the prophets, more in Moses ... and still more in Christ as in a temple.[13]

The little we know about Paul of Samosata is hardly sufficient to state with certainty what the motives or interests were behind his Christological position. Perhaps a simple surmise is permissible. What in his position would be offensive to a Jew aside from the identification of Jesus as the last and greatest prophet? I think the answer is simple. *Nothing* should be offensive for a Jew, for here Christ is relegated to the category of a prophet, even though He is said to be the last and greatest, and as such unique. God's Logos is deprived of its hypostatic nature and safely enfolded with God as an impersonal, divine attribute, a power within God without any personal existence.[14]

Was Paul of Samosata driven by the desire to formulate a Christology that was defendable from a Jewish monotheistic point of view? Or was it a longing to protect a Hellenistic concept of the divine, that God can not suffer—a view which produces the same result? We can only guess.

In any case, with Paul of Samosata we see the contours of a Christological model that would later come to characterize the Antiochene School. Christ is thought of as a true human being in the sense that He would be a true human being even without the indwelling Logos. We are dealing with a Christology of the "indwelling" type in which one understands Jesus to be a fully human individual in whom the Logos comes to dwell. This human individual would have his own integrity even without this indwelling. When Paul of Samosata speaks of Christ having two completely separated natures, he anticipates the great Antiochene theologians of the fourth and fifth centuries whose doctrine would be forever associated with the name of Nestorius. We also perceive the contours of the Christological problem or question of the Council of Chalcedon in 451. The point of this model is that the Logos unites with a *completely* human being, with an *individual* human being. This individual human being would remain even if the indwelling Logos were removed from it. Aloys Grillmeier[15] calls the Antiochene Christological model *Logos-anthropos Christology* (*anthropos:* human being). It is an apt designation that we will find useful in what follows.

Christology in the East: Alexandria

Where in the East are the opponents of Antioch that have been repeatedly mentioned? What stood opposite Antiochene theology? I believe the answer must be twofold: partly in Alexandria and partly in Ephesus (neither of which automatically agree with each other theologically).

First we look at the Alexandrian tradition. The representatives of this tradition succeeded in condemning Paul of Samosata for heresy in 268 and having him banished. Their most telling argument was that Paul of Samosata's prophet-Christology did not do justice to the incarnation. They said in effect, "It does not say in John 1:14 that the Logos dwelt in a human being but that the Word *became* flesh, became a human being."

To the question, "What would be left of the incarnate Christ if one took away the Logos," Paul of Samosata would no doubt answer, "A mere human being (*psilos anthropos*)—but nothing less either!" However, the Alexandrians answered that what would be left would be *a de-souled body* (*sôma apsychon*).

Among the Alexandrians who contended against Paul, we meet for the first time a Christological view that would continue for a long time to characterize the Alexandrian tradition, a model that Grillmeier calls the *Logos-sarx* model (*sarx*, flesh).[16] Bishop Apollinarius (361–90) expresses this model most simply and consistently, saying that the Logos in Christ took the place which the soul (more precisely, the reasoning-soul) occupies in an ordinary human being. While an ordinary person consists of soul and flesh, Christ was composed of Logos and flesh. If one imagined the Logos being removed from the incarnated One, what remained was lifeless flesh—which is what happened when Christ died.

Apollinarius: Bishop of Laodicea in Syria from 361. A friend of Athanasius and a defender of the Nicene Creed. His theory about the Logos taking the place of the reasoning-soul in Christ was condemned at the Council of Constantinople in 381. He died ca. 390.

This was how Apollinarius explained that the preexistent Logos and the incarnated Christ were one and the same subject; the same Logos-subject was active the whole time. Therefore, the common subject identity in the second article of the baptismal confession was no problem for Apollinarius (or any of the other Alexandrians).

We now note one of Grillmeier's most important points in his large work on Christology: The Logos-sarx model is shared by *all* typical Alexandrians, including the two polarities in the Arian Controversy (318–ca. 380): Athanasius and Arius. Both fall within the

Logos-sarx model![17] The Arian Controversy therefore was not just an Eastern phenomenon but, more accurately stated, an intra-Alexandrian clash.

By consistently supporting the full subject-identity between the preexistent Logos and the incarnated One—or, to phrase it in modern terms, between the agent of creation and the historical Jesus— the Alexandrians encountered the offense of the incarnation at a different juncture than did Paul of Samosata and the later Antiochenes. They solved the problem by splitting Christ's attributes so that the Logos could not be identified with anything that was part of earthly human beings who were born, grew up, became hungry and thirsty, cried, and suffered and died. The Alexandrians could not divide Christ in this manner. For them the Logos was Jesus' soul, His self, His life principle.

But then the question arose, Could such a human life principle, involved in human weakness, finitude, suffering and death, really be completely divine? Arius answered *no*.

Arius: Presbyter in Alexandria, representative of the Alexandrian Logos-sarx position. From ca. 318, after he insisted that the Logos was *created* and was not of the essence of the Father, he was involved in an intense struggle about the essence of the Logos.

The Logos, which was incarnate in Jesus, was without a doubt preexistent, said Arius, agreeing with the theological tradition and baptismal confession that considered the Logos to be an agent of creation. But the Logos itself had been created, Arius said; the Logos' uniqueness over against the rest of creation rested in that the Logos was created directly without any other agent of creation or intermediary, while the rest of creation was created with the Logos Himself as the intermediary creative agent.

While Paul of Samosata and the Antiochenes after him had problems with the subject identification in the second article of the baptismal confession, Arius strongly advocated the subject identification—and thus appeared to be a "strong" incarnation theologian.[18] But to do so, he felt he had to deny the full divinity of the Logos.[19]

What was the background for this Alexandrian Logos-sarx

schema? I believe I can safely say that it is one of the great unsolved questions about the Early Church's Christological history. The fact is that nearly all the Alexandrian theologians considered Origen (ca. 220–50) to be their great theological mentor. But Origen's theology did not fall within the Logos-sarx schema.

Origen was probably born in Alexandria ca. 185. He worked as a catechist in the congregation until ca. 215 when he had to move to Caesarea in Palestine. After a renewed stay in Alexandria (217–30), he moved permanently to Caesarea, where he founded a famous library. He was arrested and tortured during the Decian persecution (250–51). He died a few years later at the age of seventy.

Major Works: *First Principles* (*Peri archôn*), his major systematic work. *Contra Celsum,* the longest Christian apologetic work up to that time. *Sermons and Commentaries* which cover large sections of the Bible; not all are extant.

Christology:
As the Wisdom of God (Prov. 8:22ff, Wis. 7:22ff), Christ is God's image (*eikon*) from everlasting to everlasting, having proceeded from God in an "eternal birth," an ongoing generation. He contains in Himself God's creative thought and functions as the agent of creation. Origen's "image" concept explains why his Christology contained two contradictory tendencies that would generate sharp debate and unrest among his followers: Christ as God's image can be understood to mean that Christ is in every regard *like God* so that the image is identical with the original. But it can also be understood in the sense that Christ is *only* an image of God and in a certain sense *less* than God. Both of these tendencies are found in Origen. During the Arian Controversy both sides could cite selected passages in Origen in their own defense.

Origen followed a third schema: The Logos, whom Origen had undoubtedly explicitly discussed as *consubstantial* (*homoousios*) with the Father,[20] was born of the Father in an eternal, timeless "birthing," and united Himself with a preexistent human soul.

Through the incarnation, both were united with a human body. Later this Christ-soul concept was completely abandoned in Alexandrian Christology. No one knows for certain why.[21] In Origen, it functioned as a sort of buffer concept so that the Logos in Christ was prevented from attaining a too intimate participation in the suffering, weakness, etc. In later Alexandrian Christology, this buffer was lacking. Then it became necessary, as in Arius, to remove this offense by conceiving of the Logos as created; or as in Athanasius, to insist upon the offense. In any case, this Alexandrian Christology involved a mode of thinking that made the personal union (subject unity of Christ) easy to maintain. There was no separate, personal *ego* in the incarnate Christ. His ego was the ego of the Logos. The active and speaking subject in the earthly work of providing salvation was the Logos that united itself to human flesh and employed it as His instrument.

As mentioned, perhaps the most consistent representative of this Christological type (those who held to the substantial unity with the Father) was Apollinarius. He introduces us to a characteristic concept that was to become historic: the idea of nature (*physis*) as central to Christology—but a "nature" meaning a living essence that has its life principle within itself.[22] A "nature" is a self-animating, living essence (*zôon autokinêton*) that can exist by itself because its life principle is within itself. Obviously, in this context the human flesh of Christ is not a "nature." The flesh has its life principle in the Logos which has united itself with it. It is the whole Christ which is one nature; and He is just one nature, not two. On the basis of these presuppositions, the phrase "Christ is one nature" becomes a way of expressing His personal unity. (Those who most consistently carried the Alexandrian tradition further found it very difficult to reconcile themselves to statements about two natures in Christ. We know them later as *Monophysites,* who thought of themselves as the legitimate successors of the venerable tradition from Nicea, Athanasius, and the great Cyril, as noted below).

Clearly from the above, the Council of Nicea's creed (A.D. 325) did not address some important Christological conflicts—e.g., the Antiochene and Alexandrian models as to how to understand the incarnation. The settlement at Nicea sharpened rather than lessened the problem. A hundred years later, the problem still persisted and had to be addressed at the church councils at Ephesus in 431 and at Chalcedon in 451.

The two Christological models just discussed (Logos-anthropos in Antioch and Logos-sarx in Alexandria) help in understanding the broad outline of the Christological struggles before Nicea until after Chalcedon. But that does not get at the whole story. One more major Christological view in the East must be included: *Ephesus*— even though that introduces new features into what was until now a relatively simple picture. (In addition, Western Christology must be considered as well.)

Christology in the East: "Ephesus"

Quotation marks around "Ephesus" indicate that this tradition is not limited to Ephesus but embraces the surrounding region nearly congruous with the Roman province of Asia, including important ecclesiastical centers, such as Smyrna and Sardis, and some lesser ones comprising just about the seven cities in the book of Revelation to which letters were sent. Not only do these letters witness to the close fellowship between these cities, but we also have the letters of Ignatius sent to congregations in the same region.

A remark about Ignatius is necessary here. I have the impression from reading his letter to Ephesus and the other surrounding cities that, quite different from his letter to the Romans, Ignatius is writing to old acquaintances. In the letter to the Philadelphians, Ignatius mentions that in his absence several of the Asian congregations have sent bishops and deacons to Antioch (*Phila. 10*) and recommends that Polycarp convene a meeting in Smyrna to select an emissary to go to Antioch (*To Polycarp 7f*)—as though Ignatius has high hopes that the emissary from Asia will be able to guide the shepherdless Antiochenes on the right path. Thus one is led to ask, Had Ignatius previously made the same trip? Were his personal and theological roots in Asia Minor? Obviously, my opinion is yes. There are good grounds for characterizing Ignatius as *theologically* "Ephesian." And, I believe that Ignatius, Melito of Sardis (ca. 175) and Irenaeus belong together in a common Christological model that is neither Antiochene nor Alexandrian but Ephesian.

First, a striking peculiarity common to these three authors: They are reluctant to use philosophical terminology (technical or popular) in developing their Christology; they are much more at home quoting Scripture passages and employing Biblical imagery. My impression is that they deliberately express the faith in a manner as close as possible to the average person in the congregation, at least when compared to the learned theologians from Alexandria and Antioch.

As others elsewhere, both Ignatius and Irenaeus (and, one can assume, Melito also[23]) presuppose wisdom Christology. What uniquely characterizes them (especially Ignatius and Melito) is that, on the basis of a seemingly "naive" and unencumbered wisdom Christology, they can get right to the point and speak of Christ as God: Christ was God in a human being. Analagous to Grillmeier's two types, we can speak about a third type, a *theos-anthropos* type. These authors speak so freely about Jesus as God that a superficial reading of them can easily lead one to surmise that the Father and the Son are identical. This is especially true of Melito.

> He [Christ] is all things:
> inasmuch as He judges, Law;
> inasmuch as He teaches, Word;
> inasmuch as He saves, Grace;
> inasmuch as He begets, Father;
> inasmuch as He is begotten, Son;
> inasmuch as He suffers, Sheep;
> inasmuch as He is buried, Man;
> inasmuch as He is raised, God. (*On Pascha 9*)[24]

> For as a Son born, and as a lamb led, and as a sheep slain, and as a man buried, He rose from the dead as God, being by nature God and Man. (*On Pascha 8*)[25]

> He who hung the earth is hanging [on the cross];
> He who fixed the heavens has been fixed [on the cross];
> He who fastened the universe has been fastened to a tree;
> the Sovereign has been insulted; God has been murdered;
> the King of Israel has been put to death. . . . (*On Pascha 96*)[26]

Melito: Probably a bishop in Sardis; at least he was buried there. He was considered as one of the great teachers in the Asia Minor church and was a prolific author. Unfortunately, only a fragment of his works has been preserved. In 1936, Campbell Bonner identified his *Homily on the Passion.* Its

---

89

date can be fixed with great certainty at A.D. 160–70.

Several commentators have felt that Melito comes dangerously close to modalist thinking. But it is not difficult to find other passages that reveal that he was fully cognizant of the separation between the Father and the Son, even in the preexistence. Melito nowhere explicitly identifies the Father and the Son. His excessiveness in rhetoric must be taken into account, and not all of his statements are to be taken as dogmatic definitions. However, it is striking how much more direct and uninhibited Melito speaks about the suffering of God than any other author (with the exception of Ignatius).

> *Modalism:* The teaching that the Father, Son and Holy Spirit are only three different modes (*modi*) in which the one and same God appears. As understood by their opponents, modalists said that God appeared in only one of these roles at a time, so that heaven was empty when God was on earth in the form of the Son. But it is uncertain whether modalists really held to this. Known representatives of modalism included the presbyter from Asia Minor, *Noetus,* and Bishop *Sabellius* (ca. 200–220), after whom modalism in the Early Church was usually called *Sabellianism.*

I would characterize this theology as uninhibited speech about Jesus as God which at times can sound almost modalistic, and as bold talk about the Son of God's passion and death that seems almost untouched by the Greek dogma of God's immutability.

How does Irenaeus fit into this picture? First, even if Irenaeus is from Asia Minor, he is at the same time a man with a broad horizon and many contacts. We know from Eusebius, for example, that Irenaeus' opinion carried weight in Rome. Therefore we can not presume to find one pure local tradition in Irenaeus' theology. So one notices with all the more interest the bold incarnation theology which in many ways reminds one of Ignatius and Melito.[27]

Some say that He [Christ] merely suffered in outward appearance, being naturally impassible (*Against Heresies* 3.16.2).[28]

[Other Gnostics contend that Jesus suffered, but not the heavenly aeon "Christ," who at His baptism, took up His dwelling in him.] Paul, speaking to the Romans, declares, "Much more they who receive abundance of grace and righteousness for eternal life shall reign by one, Christ Jesus" (Rom. 5:17). It follows from this that he knew nothing of that Christ who flew away from Jesus [before His passion]; nor did he know of the "Savior" above, whom they hold to be impassible. For if, in truth, the one [Jesus] suffered, and the other [Christ] remained incapable of suffering (*impassibilis,*) and the one was born, but the other descended upon Him who was born, and left Him again, it is not one [Jesus Christ], but two, that are shown forth. But that the apostle did know Him as one, who both was born and who suffered, namely Christ Jesus, he again says in the same Epistle, "Know ye not, that so many of us as were baptized in Christ Jesus were baptized into His death? that like as Christ rose from the dead, so should we also walk in newness of life"(Rom. 6: 3–4; *Against Heresies* 3.16.9).[29]

[The Gnostics who divide the incarnated one into "Jesus" and "Christ"], being ignorant that His only-begotten Word, who is always present with His own creation, according to the Father's pleasure, and who became flesh, is Himself

Jesus Christ our Lord,
who did also suffer for us,
and rose again on our behalf,
and who will come again in the glory of His Father,
to raise up all flesh, and for the manifestation of salvation. . . .

There is therefore, as I have pointed out, one God the Father, and one Christ Jesus, who came by means of the whole dispensational arrangements, and gathered together all things in Himself. But in every respect, too, He is man, the formation of God; and thus He took up man into Himself, the invisible becoming visible, the incomprehensible being made comprehensible, the impassible becoming capable of suffering (*passibilis*), and the Word being made man, thus summing up all things in Himself: so that, as in super-celestial, spiritual, and invisible things, the Word of God is supreme, so also in things visible and corporeal He might possess the supremacy, and, taking to Himself the preeminence, as well as constituting Himself head of the church, He might draw all things to Himself at the proper time (*Against Heresies* 3.16.6).[30]

Grillmeier notes that Irenaeus, without eliminating the human soul in Christ, often can express the dynamic unity in the incarnated One by speaking about Logos and sarx in Christ in a manner similar

91

to the Alexandrian model.[31] There no doubt is a clear relationship between the Ephesian tradition and the later Alexandrian type. Dynamic incarnation Christology typifies the Alexandrian theologians a decade after Origen's death but could hardly have been influenced by him. Were they influenced by Irenaeus and the tradition he represented? Ephesus and Alexandria were allied even as late as the fifth century in the struggle with Nestorius and the Antiochenes. That is hardly a coincidence. It was specifically in Ephesus with its authoritative Johannine tradition and the grave of Mary [!] that the veneration of Mary developed, "she who bore God" *(theotokos).* Such talk was an abomination for Antiochenes; but for those who lived and breathed in the type of piety that Ignatius, Melito or Irenaeus represented, it must have seemed quite natural.

Christology in the West: Rome and Carthage

The picture in the West can be simplified somewhat: Rome seemed related to the Asia Minor tradition, while Carthage (e.g., Tertullian) tended to lean in the direction of Antioch. Who represents Rome is a more complicated matter. It is well known that Tertullian was ill at ease over the Roman bishops giving their blessing to Praxeas, who had come from Asia Minor and who, according to Tertullian, identified the Father and the Son in a manner—again following Tertullian—that made the Father suffer on the cross *(Patripassionism).* But we do not know who Praxeas was. We know that he came from Asia Minor and that the very conservative Roman congregation listened to him and welcomed him. Others in Rome had a high regard for yet another person from Asia Minor, the presbyter Noetus. This caused Tertullian's disciple, Hippolytus, to take up his pen and write a broadside.

Several interesting questions arise that we will not discuss here. Can one suppose that both Praxeas and Noetus (were they perhaps the same person?) actually represented the little, "naive," Asia Minor tradition that we have also met in Melito? Can we suppose that Tertullian and his disciple have caricatured them quite badly? Can it be that even Sabellius has been misunderstood and caricatured? Is it possible that some Asia Minor rhetoric fell on good soil among more subtle theologians like Tertullian, and later among Origen and his disciples?[32] I will not go any farther with these questions nor come to any conclusion. But it is a fact that the Alexandrians who later defended Nicea (those whom we surmised were influenced by Asia Minor) were accused of Sabellianism precisely because they so strongly emphasized the unity between the Father and the Son.

Be that as it may. The Roman and Asia Minor tradition to which I have alluded for the most part is known only through the writings of their opponents (always a dubious source)—but there is no doubt about Tertullian's position. We have a complete work of his, *Against Praxeas,* devoted solely to Christology. The other dogmatic works of Tertullian are rich source materials as well.[33]

Tertullian is regarded as the founder of ecclesiastical Latin. He was a layperson who had no doubt served as a catechist in his home congregation in Carthage. Toward the end of his life, he went over to the Montanist movement. From the time of his conversion to Christianity around 190 until his death in 220, his writing covered an unusually wide range of works, encompassing both theological and moral issues, as well as being a strong apologist for Christianity.

Major Works:

Apology: A classic defense of Christian monotheism against heathendom.

Against Marcion: Five books written ca. A.D. 207.

Against Hermogenes: Hermogenes was a Gnostic. Tertullian also defends the Christian belief in creation.

Against the Valentinians: Anti-Gnostic writing.

On the Flesh of Christ: Defends the reality of the incarnation against Gnostic docetism.

On the Resurrection of the Flesh: Defends, as the title states, the participation of the body in salvation.

Against Praxeas: Tertullian's major Christological work.

Tertullian also leaned decidedly toward wisdom Christology, but he developed wisdom Christology in a broader and more detailed fashion than anyone before him. Of those who immediately succeeded him, only Origen dug more deeply. Two citations from Tertullian are important to read: a summary of chapters 5–8 of his work *Against Praxeas,* and a short selection from his *Apology.*

Before the world was created, even then He [God] was not
alone for He had with Him that which He possessed in Himself,
that is to say, His own reason (*ratio*) which the Greeks call Logos.
With this Logos/Reason, God entered into an inner dialogue about
the things He planned to create, just as human beings, created in
the image of God, have an inner conversation with themselves
with the help of reason's word. In Scripture this is called God's
Word, His Wisdom, as Wisdom herself says in Prov. 8:22–31. It is
evident from this passage that Wisdom is an independent personage in and with God. When God created the world, the Word
[Logos] proceeded out of God as an external creative speech.
Therefore the Word Himself asssumes His own form and glorious
garb, His own sound and vocal utterance, when God says, "Let
there be light." This is the perfect nativity of the Word.[34] While
He is spoken of in Prov. 8:22ff as Wisdom, He is referred to as
Word and Spirit in Psalm 33:6. By His word the heavens were
established, and all the powers thereof by His Spirit, that is to say,
by the Spirit [or Divine Nature] which was in the Word. Thus it
is evident that it is one and the same power, which in one place
is described under the name of Wisdom and in another passage
under the appellation of Word. Nor need we dwell any longer on
this point, as if it were not the very Word Himself, who is spoken
of under the name both of Wisdom and of Reason, and of the
entire Divine Soul and Spirit. He became also the Son of God and
was begotten when He proceeded forth from Him. Do you then
[you ask], grant that the Word is a certain substance, constructed
by the Spirit and the communication of Wisdom? Certainly I do.
But you will not allow Him to be really a substantive being, by
having a substance of His own; in such a way that He may be
regarded as an objective entity.[35] If anyone concludes from this
that I am thinking of the Logos proceeding from the Father as an
emanation (*probole*) such as the Gnostics do when they set forth
aeon from aeon, then so be it. The concept is not unusable even
if Gnostics employ the term. Truth must not refrain from the use
of the term, its reality, and meaning, simply because heresy also
employs it. As I use the term, it signifies that the Son is an emanation from the Father, without being separated from Him. For
the root and the tree are distinctly two things, but correlatively
joined; the fountain and the river are also two forms, but indivi-
sible; so likewise the sun and the ray are two forms, but coherent

ones as also the Paraclete teaches.[36] For these substances are emanations from the substances from which they proceed. So ought one to think of the Father and the Son. They are two but simultaneously inseparable.[37]

Tertullian speaks for himself in a concise summary found in his *Apology,* chapter 21:

> First, I shall discuss His [Jesus'] essential nature, so the nature of His birth will be understood. We have already asserted that God made the world and all that it contains, by His Word, and Reason, and Power. It is abundantly plain that your philosophers, too, regard the Logos, that is, the Word and Reason, as the Creator of the universe. . . . In like manner we hold that the Spirit is the essence of the Word and Reason and Power whereby God made everything. We have been taught that [the Word etc.] proceeds from God and that through this procession He is generated so that He is the Son of God and is called God from the unity of substance with God. For God, too, is a spirit. Even when the ray is shot from the sun, it is still part of the parent mass; the sun will still be in the ray, because it is a ray of the sun. There is no division of substance, but merely an extension. Thus Christ is Spirit of Spirit, and God of God, as light of light is kindled. . . . So too, that which has come forth out of God is at once God and the Son of God, and the two are one. In this way also, as He is Spirit of Spirit and God of God, He is made a second in manner of existence— in position, not in nature. . . . This ray of God, then, as it was always foretold in ancient times, descending into a certain virgin and made flesh in her womb, is in His birth God and man united. The flesh formed by the Spirit is nourished, grows up to manhood, speaks, teaches, works, and is the Christ![38]

It is not difficult to see that Tertullian in many ways anticipates the position that the Council of Nicea was later to arrive at, even though his Stoic-tinged concept of substance is more material than the Platonic concept of essence we later meet in the Alexandrians.[39]

But Tertullian wants to avoid at all cost a possible conclusion, that of the Father suffering in the Son because of their common substance. He therefore develops in his work against Praxeas an incarnation Christology that reminds one of the Antiochenes. He distinguishes sharply between the Spirit and flesh of Christ. Only the flesh partook in suffering and weakness.

The property of each nature is so wholly preserved, that the Spirit on the one hand did all things in Jesus suitable to itself, such as miracles, and mighty deeds, and wonders; and the flesh, on the other hand, exhibited affections that belong to it. It was hungry under the devil's temptation, thirsty with the Samaritan woman, wept over Lazarus, was troubled even unto death, and at last actually died.[40]

When Jesus cried on the cross, "My God, My God, why have You forsaken Me?" it was the flesh, the soul, the voice of a human being, not that of the Word or Spirit, not the voice of God, that was heard, says Tertullian. Jesus cried out like that in order to demonstrate that God (i.e., the Father) was *impassibilis* (*Against Praxeas*, 30).[41]

To speak of the two natures almost as independently acting subjects (an abomination in the ears of Alexandrians) was to become a distinguishing feature of Western Christology as it followed in the path of Tertullian. Nor did it very much please the Antiochenes who in their own way also wished to preserve the integrity of Christ. Western Christology never reached the same level of reflection and precision on this question as in the East. But it was clear from Tertullian that Western Christology could never become monophysite. In spite of its vulnerable and somewhat dialectic formulation, Tertullian's Christology gives the impression of being in the Christological *center* where Easterners through Nicea and Chalcedon also situated themselves—a pretty good recommendation for a lonely pioneer of Latin Christology! The fact that the West has neither a Nicea nor a Chalcedon with their accompanying struggles and schism is in no small measure due to Tertullian.[42]

A short summary: The second article of the confession of faith has characteristic differences between Eastern and Western churches. The West held a simple messianic Christology, centering around the concept of Jesus as the fulfillment of messianic prophecies.

In the East, wisdom Christology dominates. The agent of creation became a human being and came to redeem His own creation. In this position, the offense of the incarnation is strongly maintained—and in a more subtle understanding of the mystery of the incarnation a division of opinion took place which had to be fought through by the Eastern theologians. Antioch tended in the direction of a *prophet Christology* in which Christ was thought of as completely inspired by God's (impersonal) Wisdom. In reaction to this, a Christology evolved among the Alexandrian theologians in which the Logos was viewed as the person-constituting element in Jesus, analagous to the soul in other human beings. We met a third Christological type in Asia Minor represented by Ignatius, Melito, and Irenaeus. They held that Jesus is "God in a human being." In the great struggles of the fifth century sharp differences arose between Antiochene Christology on the one side and Alexandrian and Asia Minor Christology on the other. But before that occurred, an internal struggle developed within the Alexandrian tradition—the struggle surrounding Arius (see the following chapter).

In the Western church, Rome leaned toward Asia Minor's *modalistic* Christology, while Tertullian in Carthage delivered a strong protest against what he saw as an identification of the Father and the Son. Tertullian's position had some similarities to the later Antiochene two-nature Christology.

The Nicene Confession of Christ

The Arian Controversy

It all began in Alexandria about A.D. 318 in a public debate between Bishop Alexander and one of his presbyters, Arius. As is so often the case, who started the debate can be argued back and forth. Both parties contended not only that the other party began it but was also chiefly responsible for the intense polemic that eventually characterized the disagreement which in the course of a few years resounded throughout the Eastern church. In a letter to his friend, Bishop Eusebius of Nicomedia, Arius took the position that the onset of the struggle occurred after Alexander had used some highly provocative expressions regarding the unity of the Son with the Father, which in Arius' eyes were clearly Sabellian and which broke completely with the orthodox Origen tradition that Arius felt duty bound to defend and which he felt certain other leading theologians would defend as well. In a sermon Alexander had said that the Father and the Son were equally eternal: "The Son is (always) unborn in the Father. He is born outside of time, born to be unborn.[1] The Father is not outside the Son, neither in our thoughts or in time. There is always the Father, always the Son. The Son is from God Himself."[2] Arius thought that Alexander not only broke significantly with the tradition from Origen which clearly subordinated the Son to the Father; worse yet, by using such expressions about the Son, Alexander erased the separation between the Father and the Son (according to Arius). Fundamental to Origen's definition of God was the concept of "that which is without a beginning." Arius contended that logically, when it came to such a category, there was room for only one, and that was the Father.[3] If it belongs to the definition of Father not to have an origin, then it cannot be that the Son is without a beginning, but He has his origin in the Father. If that is the case, then the Father is "before" the Son, at least logically. Arius further contended that, since philosophically cultured persons recognized that nothing else existed eternally except that which according to its nature was eternal, therefore to determine the Son's true nature one had to say at least that there was a time (or a "once upon a time" before time was created) when the Son did not exist.

Arius had several grievances also against the traditional Christology (as represented by Alexander) which presupposed that an attribute of God, His Wisdom or Logos, while it was at the same time God's Wisdom, was its own *hypostasis* which could become incarnated in a human being, as well as suffer, without affecting God. Arius regarded this as philosophically and theologically absurd.[4] God's Wisdom, His Logos, can not be separated from God as a separate *hypostasis*. It is, from eternity to eternity, God's own "inner" wisdom and never becomes anything else. God's essence can not be divided as though He were material. Therefore, the preexistent Wisdom-Logos which was incarnated in Jesus is *not* identical with God's own Wisdom and Logos, but has been made wise through God's own wisdom. Thus it can be said of the incarnated one that He grew in years and wisdom.

For Arius, the whole basis for traditional wisdom Christology burst into pieces. He viewed the understanding of *hypostasis*, as it had been traditionally understood, as a philosophical monstrosity and a rational impossibility. Stated more bluntly, the only use Arius had for the traditional wisdom Christology was the verb "created" in the common Greek translation of Prov. 8:22.[5] The great liberal historian of dogma, Adolf von Harnack, had a keen insight into Arius' break with tradition and his introduction of a new point of view.

> Arianism is a *new teaching* [Harnack's emphasis] in the church. . . . It is not just new because one contended so sharply and publicly that the Logos was created and was changeable, but it is new because one explicitly denies every substantive connection between the Logos and the Father. The old images which were nearly as old in the church as the Logos doctrine itself, the spring and the brook, the sun and the light, the original picture and its reflection, are here cast away. It signifies nothing less than that the Christian doctrine of the Logos and God's Son is discarded. All that remains, are the old names.[6]

Arius was recognized by his contemporaries, both his friends as well as his opponents, as being philosophically and theologically astute and superior to his bishop, Alexander, who no doubt had an instinctive perception that there lay in Arius a fundamental rejection of traditional Christology. (One can not help giving Alexander his due in that regard.)

Now and then Arius is miscast as a conservative theologian who sought to return to the pre-Origen tradition and as a renewer of apologetic Christology. But to properly evaluate Arius, we need to understand how the earlier Christology considered the starting point in the relationship between the Father and the Son (i.e., the emanation of the Son or of being begotten of the Father). The earliest documents are somewhat brief on these points but not entirely silent. Neither are the Jewish writings that form the backdrop. While in Proverbs 8 a picture of a *birth* dominates, chapter 7 of the Wisdom of Solomon speaks rather in ways that encourage thinking of the relationship as *outpouring* or emanation.

The Christian writers who first touch upon the subject (Justin and Tertullian) seem to be closest to emanation thinking. Justin uses the illustration of a fire setting new fires to argue that God Himself does not contain less Logos because the Logos proceeded from Him as a separate *hypostasis*.[7] Tertullian uses the same illustration (as well as the other emanation pictures of Wisdom such as the brook running out of the spring, the tree shooting up from the root). He explicitly uses the technical word *outpouring* (*probolē*), in spite of the fact that it was one of the Gnostic catch phrases. He can say that the Son is "a part of and a derivation" of the Father's substance.[8]

For Eastern theologians this must have sounded dangerously physical or material. But when they had placed sufficient reservations against such misunderstandings, they found that they basically thought the same way: The Logos is like God's own Wisdom, the Son, and in an unfathomable and ineffable manner is *derived* from the Father, from His own essence. God can therefore never be thought of without the Son, for that would mean that God was without His Wisdom; and that would be absurd. The analogy from *Wisdom 7* is frequently used and strongly emphasized: Light is never without its rays, its *apaugasma*. The rays of light share in the same essence as light. This way of depicting the relationship between the Father and the Son is unqualifiably found in the wisdom type, in the concept of an hypostasized divine attribute. All the important pre-Nicene theologians who wrote on Christology thought in this manner. I contend that we here have a line of tradition that goes back in unbroken succession to the main wisdom Christological passages of the New Testament itself.

Arius broke with this tradition because he maintained that it is philosophically meaningless and untenable. He rejected explicitly all talk about emanations from God and emphatically rejected the old illustration of the fire that lights another fire.[9] Harnack is obviously correct when he states that Arianism represented a radical departure from the Christological tradition.

But now let us return to Alexandria and the struggle between Arius and his bishop. The Emperor Constantine had just tried to bring about unity in the Western church following the Donatist schism in North Africa and did not look favorably upon another potential schism in the East. The emperor had envisioned the church as the religiously unifying factor in the restored empire. Only one unified church could be unifying. The emperor therefore sent his ecclesiastical advisor, the Spanish bishop Hosius, on a reconciliation mission. Hosius carried a somewhat sharp letter from the emperor that criticized both parties for asking questions so difficult that they had to be considered beyond human comprehension. Said the emperor, the question which each party had asked the other ought not to have been asked, and the answers that had been given should not have been given.[10] Hosius quickly realized that these exchanges were not a basis for mediation, and when he learned what the issues were about, he himself entered into the fray. The Arian historian, Philostorgius, recounts that Alexander and Hosius—well before Nicea—quickly agreed on the main Nicene catchword "of one substance (with the Father)," *homoousios,* as well as the need to condemn Arius.[11] (Most likely, Alexander and Hosius discovered each other during Hosius' visit to Alexandria. In any case, Hosius returned home with his mission unaccomplished.)

The Council of Nicea

The emperor could not permit his intervention in Alexandria to be without results. He therefore summoned an ecumenical council to meet at Ancyra, with the intention of not allowing the theologians to return home before they had come to an agreement. Hosius and Alexander now had to make sure that peace in the church was not achieved by a forced reconciliation between the Arian and anti-Arian positions but rather by the exclusion of radical Arianism from the church. As a strategic starting point leading to the ecumenical council, Hosius arranged a smaller regional synod to meet at Antioch over New Year's in 325. The unambiguous anti-Arian confession[12] which was adopted reads like an echo of a previous letter of Alexander against Arius.[13] We will return to it below. The three bishops who refused to subscribe (among them the well-known Eusebius of Caesarea, widely respected for his learning) were suspended from their bishoprics—thus anticipating the verdict from the impending ecumenical church council.

Eusebius of Caesarea: Bishop in Caesarea (Palestine) from 313 to his death in 339. The most learned theologian of his time. Among other things, wrote a *Church History*, still the most important source for ante-Nicene [pre-Nicene] church history because of his many citations from older works that are no longer extant. Eusebius became a close friend of Emperor Constantine and wrote his biography. In the Arian controversy, Eusebius occupied a mediating position. He himself was not an Arian but rather a conservative Origenist. Nevertheless, he participated in the ecclesiastical-political struggle in opposition to the Nicene party.

Perhaps Constantine realized that Hosius had begun to play too large a personal role in the negotiations and that Hosius had become dissatisfied with the way Eusebius was being handled, as the emperor (correctly) must have come to see Eusebius as a valuable and useful person. The emperor decided to have the ecumenical council assemble at Nicea, which was closer to the capital, so that he could oversee the course of the negotiations. And so 250 bishops came to Nicea with their traveling expenses paid by the emperor. The opening ceremonies were impressive with the emperor himself personally in attendance. The not so few bishops who had scarcely survived the Diocletian persecution twenty years earlier must have had problems believing what they heard and saw.

But unpleasant matters were on the agenda, and one had to take a position with regard to both Eusebius and Arius. In a post-council letter which Eusebius wrote to his diocese before he had actually reached home, he relates that he had read a statement during the council which contained his confession of faith and an assurance that such had always been his position. The emperor had quickly taken the floor and declared that Eusebius' confession was completely orthodox and in agreement with his own position. One needed only to add one word, *homoousios*. But those who drew up the final draft of the confession used this as a pretext to add much more, says Eusebius. He does not say who "those" were.[14]

Previously, historians interpreted Eusebius' statement (cited above on pages 77–78) as a confession which served as the basis for the final draft that the council drew up. Presumably, differences between Eusebius' confession and that of the council were resolved by deliberate revision and alteration. However, Hans Lietzmann has shown through a detailed comparison that this could not possibly have been the case. Rather the Nicene Creed seems to have evolved from a text close to that used by the church in Jerusalem.[15] J. N. D. Kelly also has argued convincingly that Eusebius' contention that his confession was the basis for the council's confession simply does not agree with the facts. Eusebius' creed must rather be seen in connection with his own rehabilitation and not as the first phase of the council's endeavor to draw up a new confession.[16] Eusebius' account therefore does not tell us very much about the process which lay behind the final version of the council's creedal statement.

> *Athanasius:* Participated in the Council of Nicea as a young deacon. Succeeded Alexander as bishop of Alexandria (328–73). As a theologian and church bureaucrat, Athanasius appeared to be the most uncompromising defender of the Nicene Creed, causing him to be exiled five times from his bishopric. His numerous works against the Arians constitute the first "classical" development of Eastern Christology.

Athanasius' account, which has often been neglected unfairly in historical research, does reveal a great deal about the process.[17] The picture that Athanasius presents regarding the origin of the Nicene Creed is described in two stages. First, the editorial committee (if we dare call it such) presented a creed that contained only the words and expressions found in Scripture; that is to say, it avoided the later contested terms like *essence* (*ousia* and *homoousia*). The intent of the first statement, however, was clearly anti-Arian in this first edition of the creed. It said that the Son was "from God," that He was the Logos and Wisdom, that He was not a creature (*ktisma*) or a work (*poiêma*), but the Father's own offspring (*gennêma*). Looking more carefully at this first edition, one is impressed by two things. First, this confession expresses the church's old wisdom Christology in Scripture's own words. It is a *conservative* confession. Second, several words and turns of expression remind one of the confession from the Synod at Antioch held several months before, where Alexander and his supporters undoubtedly set the agenda.[18] In other words, it seems as though the same (or several of the same) men were also responsible for the first version at Nicea when everything (probably) went according to Hosius' and Alexander's direction. Eusebius refers to them only with the impersonal pronoun. (After all, he could hardly offend the emperor's ecclesiastical advisor!)

When this first anti-Arian draft was presented to the church assembly for discussion, something amazing occurred. The Arians took the wind out of the balloon by declaring that they were in agreement with the creed that had been submitted! They found that all the words used of the Son, could pertain also to creatures. (Note, however, that some of the Scripture passages they alluded to in this connection, such as the use of the word *power* in relation to grasshoppers and larvae in Joel 2:25, are not the kind that one thinks of spontaneously.) It seems as though the Arians were well prepared to counter these formulations and that they had had several months to map out a strategy as to how they ought to tackle a new creed similar to the one presented at Antioch. Athanasius states that the Arians whispered and blinked to each other when they were presented with the first draft. The editorial committee felt forced to present a new creed that removed all ambiguity. Where it previously had stated that the Son was "from God," it now was clarified with the words "from the substance of the Father" and "of one Being with the Father" (*homoousion tô Patri*), which remain in the Nicene Creed until this day. The first of these amplifications is explicitly introduced with the words, "That is to say"! The text reads as follows:

And (we believe) in one Lord Jesus Christ,
the Son of God,
begotten from the Father, only-begotten,
that is, from the substance of the Father,
God from God,
light from light,
true God from true God,
begotten not made,
of one substance with the Father,
through whom [the Son] all things came into being,
things in heaven and things on earth,
Who because of us men and because of our salvation
came down and became incarnate,
becoming man,
suffered
and rose again on the third day,
ascended to the heavens,
will come to judge the living and the dead.

But as for those who say, There was when He was not, and before being born He was not, and that He came into existence out of nothing, or who assert that the Son of God is of a different hypostasis or substance, or is subject to alteration or change—these the Catholic and apostolic Church anathematizes.[19]

Looking more closely, it is evident that the editorial committee in the last draft abandoned the procedures they had followed at Antioch. They did not wish any longer to formulate a relatively detailed independent confession of faith but rather were content with a simple baptismal confession such as all were accustomed to from their worship services but with a few unambiguous amplifications (italicized in the passage above). Article two of the baptismal confession had hitherto consisted only of a series of Scriptural allusions and citations. Now it contained a minimal amount of Scriptural interpretation as well. This interpretation resulted in the inclusion of the words *substance* and *of one substance,* which clearly were meant to be conceptual expressions for the old illustrations (Scriptural illustrations!) of the sun which allows its rays to proceed from itself, light that reflects its own brilliance, roots that send forth a tree, and the spring which allows the brook to flow from itself. When Athanasius explains what *substance* connotes, he falls back on these Scriptural images; and when he explains what the illustrations mean, he latches on to the concepts. It is clear that they are meant to throw light mutually on each other. Tertullian does something very similar in using the term *substance* as a commentary and explanation of what is contained in Scripture's illustrations of wisdom's procession from the Father (*Against Praxeas 8*).

Notice that the statement about the Son "being of one substance" with the Father, at the end of the interpolations, affirms what the confession has already expressed clearly enough. The bishops clearly knew that *homoousios* was a risky word to use. It had an encumbered history: the Gnostics had used it; the Manicheans had used it; the heresiarch, Paul of Samosata, had used it;[20] nor was it to be found in Scripture. Many felt that the term smacked of Sabellianism: that the Father is the same *hypostasis* as the Son. (At this time they had not yet come to an accepted terminological difference between *hypostasis* and *substance*; therefore, without doubt *homoousios* could be interpreted in a Sabellian manner.) Nevertheless, the bishops used the term for at least two reasons: The emperor had mentioned it, employed it against materialist misunderstandings, and he specifically requested that it be included. But equally important, all knew that a consistent Arian could not swallow this word. Therefore the phrase was incorporated into the creed with great care. First, the other interpolations clearly indicate how the word *homoousios* was to be understood. It was not to be interpreted in a Sabellian manner (the Son is *of* the Father's substance, i.e., he is *born* of the Father) or in any other course manner. To make the whole matter impossible to misunderstand, they introduced a list of condemnable Arian catchwords at the end, leaving no doubt against whom the confession was pitted or how the emotional word *homoousios* was to be understood.

The final version of the confession was very difficult for an Origenist of Eusebius' type to swallow and must have been virtually impossible for a pure Arian. When imperial pressure began to be exerted, many employed hermeneutical gymnastics and inner reservations.[21] Only two persons refused to subscribe to the new creed. The imperial reaction was relatively mild. The emperor chose banishment for those who refused to subscribe, something which he himself could always reverse at a later time (instead of a formal excommunication that could be lifted only by a new church assembly). Arius was given the same sentence—and shortly thereafter the emperor took steps to have the sentence annulled, since his long range goal was to bring about unity in the church. In Nicea he had been confronted with such a determined theological front against Arianism that he realized it was not possible to force a compromise formula on the assembly. Perhaps he did not realize just how controversial *homoousios* really was.

The Nicene Creed therefore is not the result of imperial church politics. It is a creed formulated by conservative bishops for whom the church's old Christological tradition was normative and nonnegotiable. The creedal text does not pay the slightest attention to Arius' concern about philosophical difficulties in the old wisdom Christology; they are simply ignored. When the church confesses its faith, it does not at the same time question it.

Nicea: The Incarnation and the Image of God

Those who create history seldom are cognizant of all the ramifications of their actions. The church fathers at Nicea were no exception. Their primary intention was of a conserving kind. Wanting to retain the church's old confession of Christ, they viewed Arius as introducing novelty. Seen today from a wider perspective, Nicea represents an important threshhold in Christological development. It was not insignificant that the Alexandrians, who otherwise were known as the most ardent incarnation theologians in the church, just at this point sided so unambiguously with *homoousios.* The Logos, who in their Christology was the only *ego* in the incarnated One, was identical with the Logos who was of the same substance as the Father. The paradox of the incarnation was more of a problem among the Alexandrians than among the Antiochenes because the Alexandrians could not as easily divide Jesus' works between the two natures.

We would be simplifying the picture in an unwarranted manner if we did not add that the Alexandrians also drew back from acknowledging in too direct a manner the Logos' limitations and suffering. Even Athanasius drew back from lodging Jesus' human psychology in His Logos-ego; he placed it in "the flesh" (*sarx*). Whether or not Athanasius considered this a satisfactory solution, is not easy to determine. On this point, Cyril of Alexandria (100 years later) introduced an important modification in Alexandrian

---

Cyril of Alexandria: Bishop of Alexandria from 412 to 444. An ecclesiastical and theological leader in the struggle between Alexandrian and Antiochene Christology from 428. Cyril became, alongside of Athanasius, the great "classical" exponent of Christology in the Eastern church. Later he was cited as the great authority by both the supporters of Chalcedon and the Monophysites.

Christology, speaking in his later works about the *soul* of Jesus.[22] No doubt his conflict with the Antiochenes led him in this direction. But it is also possible that impulses from another source were still more important, namely, the influence from the Cappadocian fathers, especially the two Gregorys, who appeared to take a mediating position between Athanasius and the Cappadocians.

The Cappadocians:

Basil: Monk; learned theological author; bishop of Caesarea in Cappadocia (central Asia Minor) from 370 until his death in 379. Developed the "new Nicene" Christology and trinitarian doctrine. More of an Origenist than Athanasius, yet nevertheless allied himself with the latter. Became an authority in the Eastern church especially through the monastic movement.

Gregory of Nyssa: Brother of Basil. A very important theologian. Bishop in the little Cappadocian city of Nyssa from 371 to his death in 394. Participated in the Council of Constantinopole (381).

Gregory of Nazianzus: A friend of Basil and Gregory of Nyssa. The greatest rhetorician of the three.

These three Cappadocians are often called "the new-Nicene party." In older scholarship they were often viewed as opponents of Athanasius ("the old Nicean"); however, this has been overstated. The lasting influence of the Cappadocians stems from their defense of the Nicene Creed

---

> against Sabellian misunderstanding, by distinguishing be-
> tween *ousia* (substance) and *hypostasis.* God is one sub-
> stance in three hypostases.

During the period between Nicea (325) and Constantinople (381), the Cappadocians not only effected a clarification of the terminological muddle surrounding the doctrine of the Trinity but also brought a corrective to the one-sided Logos-sarx model of the Alexandrians. The two Gregorys shaped their polemic as though it were directed against Apollinarius, while grounding it on an important concept that Origen had already formulated: If these were a part of human-ness which Christ had not taken upon Himself, that part would not have been redeemed (healed) either.[23] Former historians of dogma called this the "physical" redemption theory. The name can be argued, but the teaching of the church fathers was clear enough: Through Adam's fall, the whole human being has come under the rule and power of death, and the whole person is in need of salvation. This salvation is tied only to Jesus' passion, death, and resurrection where Jesus, as it were, leads our redeemed human nature through death into life. It is therefore important that He take with Him the *whole* of us, for that which is not assumed is not saved. The Cappadocians used this to great effect against Apollinarius. Later, Cyril thought along the same lines.

In any case, through the Cappadocians and Cyril, a subtle nuancing of the Alexandrian model takes place which allowed a larger role for Jesus' human *psyche* (His complete and undivided humanity), thus maintaining the essential concern of the Nicene Creed. He who suffered and died as a true human being was the same, identical subject as the Logos through whom God created the world and the entire human race. This Logos originated out of the Father's innermost thought. He is the Father's Wisdom, His will, His creative thought, His salvific thought. Jesus is both "from the substance of the Father" as well as "of one substance with the Father."

Perhaps unintentionally, it was precisely this combination of Alexandrian incarnation Christology and homoousian creedal identity that became epic-making in the Nicene Creed. In the long run, this creedal statement had to have implications for the concept of God.

Much pre-Nicene Christology clearly tendened to *subordinate*

Christ under the Father (in part determined by the neo-Platonic assumptions employed in the theoretical perusal of Christology). This view made it easier to speak about the suffering of the Logos than about God's suffering. (The difference was due to the Son's "divergent behavior," says Tertullian.) The Early Church fathers held that the Son, not the Father, was afoot each time Scripture said that God allowed Himself to be seen since God's theophanies (in which He had to "humiliate" Himself in order to be seen) are more easily ascribed to the Logos than to God the Father—because there was an undefined difference in degree between the Father and the Son.

In the long run, the Nicene Creed came to operate as a corrective to this tendency toward insubordination. In Nicea one said (based on the pre-Nicene wisdom Christology) *homoousios,* thereby tearing away the philosophical premise of, for example, Justin and Tertullian's mode of reasoning regarding the Son's conduct in the Old Testament theophanies. Thus Nicea brought about deep-seated consequences for the concept of God, because the incarnation could not now be excused by alluding to the Son's "divergent behavior." No, it was a Son *of the same substance as the Father* who was born, ate, drank, hungered, became thirsty, suffered and died![24]

In the Alexandrian tradition, as stated, assumptions were made that had profound consequences for the doctrine of God. In the Antiochene two-fold Christ, it was much easier to protect the concept of God's immutability untouched by the suffering of the incarnated one. It was also among the successors of the Alexandrian tradition that we later find clear expressions of God's suffering in Christ such as in Proclus of Constantinople, who stated that "One of the Trinity was crucified according to the flesh."[25]

When a person correctly visualizes the formidable implications devolved from the concept of God's immutability—for all people of antiquity, including the church's theologians—one is tempted to view such a declaration as a miracle of God which occurred in the midst of fallen humanity's theological struggle. It is a miracle that the evangelical account of the suffering Savior was not offered on the altar of Greek logic, which demanded either that Jesus was not God because He suffered, or that He had not suffered since He was God.

Studying this controversy is a double exercise in humility. It is humbling because the actors all too often appear all too human. But in a positive sense, it is humbling because one is filled with wonder and thanksgiving, and yes respect, for theologians who through all of this insisted upon and made clear the folly (for human minds) of the incarnation.

6

The Chalcedonian Definition of Christ (451)

Antioch: The Two Natures

The close of the last chapter showed how some inside the Alexandrian tradition attempted to modify the one-sided Logos-sarx typology to accommodate the point of view that "what He [God] did not assume, He did not heal." This chapter examines more closely how Christology developed in Alexandria's old opponent Antioch.

First, note that there were strong theological antagonisms within Antioch and not all theologians who came from or worked in this city were Antiochenes in the theological sense as we use the word here.[1] When speaking of the Antiochene School of the fourth and fifth centuries, four theologians stand out above all: Diodorus of Tarsus (died before 394); Theodore of Mopsuestia (died 428); Nestorius (died 451); and Theodoret of Cyrrhus (died ca. 466). The latter participated in the Council of Chalcedon and was no doubt responsible for the formula of unity between the Alexandrians and the Antiochenes to which Cyril of Alexandria subscribed in 433. It is obvious that there was a growing movement towards a kind of middle ground between the Alexandrians and the Antiochenes that led to Chalcedon. Undoubtedly, the problem of finding a unifying formula, which the Alexandrians and Antiochenes had tried to solve by themselves and with each other, was the occasion for the council.

Knowing the position of the Antiochenes is essential for understanding the Council of Chalcedon. That requires looking more closely at the Christology of Theodore of Mopsuestia.

> *Theodore of Mopsuestia:* Born, grew up, and was educated in Antioch. Bishop of Mopsuestia, 392–428. Theodore was a distinguished Biblical theologian and exegete. He was

so highly thought of that he was simply called "The Inter-preter." During his lifetime he was considered orthodox; but in the wake of the Nestorian controversy, he was labeled a heretic by the Council of Constantinople in 553.

Theodore's polemic is directed against the Arians and the Apollinarians. He especially directed his attention against the Logos-sarx typology that both Arians and Apollinarians shared.

> Arius' ... disciples say that Christ took on a body but not a soul; the divine nature, they say, takes the place of the soul. And they lower the divine nature of the Unique [Son] to the point (of saying) that He declines from His natural grandeur and performs the actions of the soul by enclosing Himself in the body and accomplishing everything to make it "subsist." Consequently, if the divinity takes the place of the soul, it (the body) had neither hunger, nor thirst, nor was it tired, nor did it have need of food; for all this happens to the body because of its weakness and be-cause the soul is not equipped to satisfy the needs which it has save according to the law of the nature which God has given it.[2]

It is important to note the line of reasoning: Why is it that we human beings hunger, cry, thirst, etc.? Because we have a limited life principle. Our soul is in itself limited and can not give directly all that our body craves. This limited life principle, the soul, is responsible for all of our human limitations.

But we see that all of these human limitations were also a part of Jesus' condition. If we are to take seriously Jesus' true humanity, it means that there is also in Jesus a human, limited, life principle, a human soul that is answerable for Jesus' human finiteness. If the Logos had been directly the non-souled body's life principle, the body would not have experienced any limitations. It would not have known hunger, thirst, etc. Theodore maintains that a consistently applied Logos-sarx Christology will result in a human nature completely absorbed by the Logos, namely, docetism.

Both Theodore and the Alexandrians stand together on the declaration that the *Logos became human*. But while the Alexandrians emphasize *became*, Theodore emphasizes *human*: Christ was a true human being with human limitations because He also assumed a limited human life principle, namely, a human soul.

In addition to this line of reasoning, Theodore applies the well-known salvation principle: That which is not assumed, is neither saved. The human soul, says Theodore, has an even greater need to be saved than the body because it is *the soul* that sins. The body has to suffer death as punishment for the sins of the soul. It is the soul that is actually the subject of sin, not the body.

> Therefore Christ had to take on not only a body but also a soul, or rather the opposite, He had to first and foremost assume a soul, and thereafter a body on account of the soul.[3]

We note that Theodore and the Alexandrians operate within the same soteriological framework, though it is probably correct to say that Theodore has a stronger moralistic character than the Alexandrians. Christ's human [created] soul reaches perfection through its union with the Logos. Grillmeier summarizes by stating, "It nonetheless remains the fact that the created soul provides the life for the body of Christ and is also the principle of the acts decisive for our redemption."[4] Or in the words of Theodore himself against Apollinarius,

> Moreover [the divine Son] furnished His cooperation in the proposed works to the one who was assumed. [Now] where does this [cooperation] entail that the Deity replaced the [human] *nous* (*sensus*) in Him who was assumed? ... Why, in the face of immediate need, did He stand in want of vehement prayers—prayers which, as the blessed Paul says, He brought before God with a loud and clamorous voice and with many tears? How was He seized of such immense fear that He gave forth fountains of sweat by reason of His great terror?[5]

"The difference between this picture of Christ and the other, that of the Logos-sarx Christology, is quite apparent. The human nature of Christ regains its real physical-human inner life and its capacity for action," the Roman Catholic, Grillmeier, states,[6] thereby revealing that some of his own sympathies lie on the side of the Antiochenes. Jesus was obedient in suffering through His identification with humanity. It was Jesus' human soul that was obedient unto death. (The Alexandrians thought rather that it was the Logos which *allowed* its flesh to suffer.)

So what about the *oneness* of Jesus? The opponents of Theodore felt that his Jesus fell apart. On the one side was the indwelling Logos and on the other side was a self-sufficient human being. Theodore was referred to as a "resurrected Paul of Samosata." That was unfair. Theodore clearly said that in the incarnation there was not just a quantitative difference from the Word dwelling in the prophets. Although the Logos did not melt together with a prophet's *ego* so as to become one person, this is what takes place in Jesus. Yet Theodore certainly seems to lack clearly defined concepts to express this amalgamation. In a commentary concerning Christ, regarding the expression "God who is over all" (Rom. 9:5), he states,

> [This reveals] the glory of Christ which comes from God the Word, who assumed Him and united Him to Himself.... And because of this exact conjunction which this man has with God the Son, the whole creation honors Him and even worships Him. Blessed Paul could doubtless have said "*in whom* is God over all," but he avoids this [way of speaking] and says "*who is God over all*," because of the exact conjunction of the two natures.[7]

There is just one *ego* in Christ; not a human-ego and a Logos-ego. What is lacking in Theodore is that this one ego remains standing as a third unified authority alongside of the two complete natures of the human and the Logos. "What he chiefly lacks is the recognition, rooted so deeply in Alexandrine intuition, that in Christ the 'Logos' is the one 'I' and the one subject."[8]

As mentioned, what is lacking are clearly defined and suitable terms for the unity of person. The term that Theodore prefers to use is *prosopon*. The usual philosophical definition of this word stated that a *prosopon* is that shape in which a nature or a *hypostasis* appears. The two natures of Christ had therefore a common mode of appearance, a common *prosopon*. Theodor uses the terminology of Chalcedon which employed both *prosopon* and *hypostasis* as concepts of unity and nature (*physis*) as distinguishing concepts. With Cyril of Alexandria, as we have seen, the term *nature* is used in an entirely different manner. Here it refers to the incarnated one's personal unity. *Nature* is the living, active person. With Theodore, we can imagine the Logos sharing His *prosopon* with the human being to whom He united himself. Human nature is absorbed into the *prosopon* of the Logos. Theodore illustrates this by comparing the unity between soul and body in a human being:

115

Man is said to consist of a soul and a body, and we say that these—soul and body—are two natures, but that one man is composed out of both. . . . The division of natures persists: the soul is one thing, the flesh another. The one is immortal while the other is mortal; the one is rational, but the other, irrational. Yet the two are one man, and one of the two [natures] is never absolutely and properly said to be "man" in itself.[9]

Body and soul each can be said to have a nature (and a *hypostasis*), but together they constitute one *prosopon*. Grillmeier concludes that Theodore's Christology is deficient in the sense that he has not yet reached the terminological and conceptual clarity reached at Chalcedon, but he is no heretic. His theology is open in the direction of Chalcedon, yes, he even can be seen as a forerunner of Chalcedon in the Eastern church's theology.

Let me in conclusion draw attention to the two uses of the term *nature* which we have met in Cyril and Theodore. With Cyril, nature is a dynamic concept, a designation for a living, active entity, a living subject. It therefore functions in his theology as a term for unity. With Theodore, as the analogy to the human body and soul indicates, nature is a much more abstract term, similar to the Western substance concept. Nature is used as a term not for the living, active person but for the respective human and divine elements in Christ. As we shall see, this also points forward toward Chalcedon.

The Nestorian Controversy

We must now look closer at the struggle surrounding the theological crisis that led to the Council of Chalcedon. It is intimately connected with Nestorius.

> *Nestorius:* A monk in Antioch; probably a pupil of Theodore of Mopsuestia. Appointed bishop of Constantinople in 428 by the emperor. Deposed by the Council of Ephesus in 431. Exiled to a monastery; to Egypt in 436 where he died ca. 451.

With Nestorius, the conflict between Alexandria and Antioch intensified as ecclesiastical politics escalated (as so often is the case).

Nestorius became bishop of Constantinople the year Theodore died (428).

> Hardly had we come here, when we discovered that some who belonged to the church were opposed to each other. Some called the holy virgin "Mother of God" (*theotokos*); others called her "Mother of man" (*anthropotokos*). I called together both parties and suggested calling her "Mother of Christ" (*kristotokos*); for this term acknowledges both sides, God and man, as it is used in the Gospel. [10]

Nestorius tried to be a mediator in a liturgical struggle over how one ought to address Mary. He felt he had found the key in solving the whole dispute. (This he never should have done, because then both sides became dissatisfied.)

Nestorius developed his Christology as a disciple of Theodore. The first polemical broadsides were directed against the Arians and the Apollinarians; the last ones included Cyril of Alexandria. Nestorius reasoned that if the Logos is the life principle of Jesus' body, then Mary quite correctly can be said to be the "Mother of God"; however, Nestorius wanted to avoid the expression in order to counter the Arians who liked the expression, because a God who was *born* could hardly be a true God.

At first glance Nestorius' term for the oneness in Christ is simply the name *Christ*. The weakness is that this one Christ-subject is hardly more than the sum of the two, each in and of themselves, complete natures. The natures are added up, so to speak, and the sum total is Christ. "Christ is the common name for the two natures." This was at least what the opponents of Nestorius understood his Christology to be. It is clear that Nestorius, in the same manner as Theodore, was seeking a mode of thought and terminology that can express the oneness in Christ and at the same time say that this oneness is something that really exists in the person Jesus so that the term "Christ" is not just a linguistic concept. The term he seized upon is the same as Theodore's *prosopon*. The word that signifies the association of the natures is *synapheia*. Nestorius did not use the term *Christ* purely as an addition concept [i.e., just putting the person Jesus and "Christ" next to each other].

In recent years, historians of dogma have questioned whether the disagreements between Nestorius and Cyril of Alexandria were as great as the two parties thought them to be.[11] Both no doubt pointed out weaknesses in the other side, but both also dealt with central issues of concern. It is perhaps fair to say that both were correct in their positive concerns. Cyril strongly championed the personal and subject unity in Christ and expresses this through a dynamic concept of nature that highlighted the personal unity of Jesus as an *active* subject. Nestorius in his own way also wanted to preserve personal unity but lacked an adequate dynamic term for it. Still, both *prosopon* and *synapheia* appear quite pale and static alongside the dynamic *one nature* of Cyril. Then again, Nestorius could vigorously maintain the true and complete humanity, while Cyril's nature concept was difficult to express terminologically.

The Council of Chalcedon (451)

When the Council of Chalcedon was called together, many must have felt that any theological advance would have to involve a clarification and common understanding of the *words* one used—and the decrees of Chalcedon do contain just such a clarification. Many have since questioned the unduly specific language and the subsequent influence that developed from this church council, but the situation in the fifth century warranted such action.

The Council of Chalcedon obviously directed its attention to more than just linguistic disagreement. The opposition between the radical disciples of Cyril and the moderate Antiochenes during the years just prior to the council had become so fierce and ecclesiastical politics had become so entrenched that a new church assembly had to have as its first priority the creation of unity and agreement in the badly torn apart Eastern church. Moreover the radical disciples of Cyril, under the leadership of Dioscorus at the "Robber Synod" in Ephesus (449), had so grossly offended the bishop of Rome that the emperor realized the unavoidable necessity of calling a new council. (We will forego further discussion of the dramatic maneuvers in ecclesiastical politics that all the parties engaged in during the years just before the council.)[12]

From Nestorius to Chalcedon

The Antiochene Tradition:	*The Alexandrian Tradition:*
"two natures"	"one nature"
428–431: *Nestorius* bishop of Constantinople. Struggle over Mary as "Mother of God."	412–444: *Cyril* bishop of Alexandria; attacks Nestorius
	431: *Council of Ephesus*, led by Cyril, condemned Nestorius
448: *Eutyches*. A radical disciple of Cyril. Condemned by *Flavian* in Constantinople because he denied that Christ was of the same substance as humanity.	449: Bishop Dioscorus of Alexandria leads a synod in Ephesus (*Robber Synod*) where Eutyches is endorsed and Flavian deposed. Flavian appeals to *Leo,* bishop of Rome.

449: *Leo* writes a doctrinal letter to Flavian in which he rejects both Eutyches and Nestorius but conceptually allies himself close to Antiochene Christology.

451: *Council of Chalcedon* acknowledges Leo's doctrinal letter [Leo's Tome] as orthodox. Formulates a moderate two-nature doctrine.

Two episodes will be recounted because they belong directly to the background for understanding the decrees of the Council of Chalcedon.

The first is the interrogation and condemnation of Eutyches, who was a radical and somewhat stubborn disciple of Cyril in Constantinople. He drove the one-nature concept to the extreme and wound up denying that Jesus had the same nature as the human race. The bishop in Constantinople, Flavian, presided at a local church synod that heard and condemned Eutyches. The protocol from this hearing has been preserved and reads in part as follows:

Flavian: Do you acknowledge Christ to be of two natures?

119

Eutyches: I have never yet presumed to speculate about the nature of my God, the Lord of heaven and earth; I admit that I have never said that He is consubstantial *[homoousios]* with us. . . . I confess that the holy Virgin is consubstantial with us, and that of her our God was incarnate. . . .

Florentius: Since the mother is consubstantial with us, then surely the Son is also?

Eutyches: Please observe that I have not said that the body of a man became the body of God, but the body was human, and the Lord was incarnate of the Virgin. If you wish me to add that His body is consubstantial with ours, I will do so; but I take the word consubstantial in such a way as not to deny that He is the Son of God. Hitherto I have altogether avoided the phrase *consubstantial after the flesh*. But I will use it now, since your Holiness demands it. . . .

Florentius: Do you or do you not admit that our Lord who is of the Virgin is consubstantial [with us] and of two natures after the incarnation?

Eutyches: . . . . I admit that our Lord was of two natures before the union, but after the union one nature. . . . I follow the doctrine of the blessed Cyril and the holy fathers and the holy Athanasius. They speak of two natures before the union, but after the union and incarnation they speak of one nature, not two.[13]

At the interrogation of Eutyches, we notice a new way of expressing the two natures of Christ through what might be called *the double homoousios*. Christ is consubstantial with the Father *and with us*. If the term *nature* revolves around this conceptualization as a more general expression of the humanity and divinity of the incarnated Christ, then it is clear that it is used in a different manner than that envisioned by Cyril. During the synod in Constantinople Flavian proposed a creedal position that contained a concept of nature which no longer was held by the followers of Cyril, being more common and abstract and in line with the Antiochene's:

We confess that Christ is *of two natures* after the incarnation, in *one* hypostasis and *one* prosopon in Christ.[14]

Nature is here no longer a concept of unity for the active person in Christ (as is so often the case in Cyril) but a more abstract term for Jesus' humanity and divinity while the terms connoting oneness are *hypostasis* and *prosopon* as well as *Christ*. This clearly anticipates

120

Chalcedon's use of those expressions and harks back to the Cappadocians' terminology.

After the condemnation of Eutyches, both sides appealed to Rome. Leo's answer is to be found in the famous *Tome to Flavian*. I will not go into any detail regarding this well-known and often commented-upon treatise,[15] except to state that Leo's position on the incarnation follows in the footsteps of Tertullian. Obviously, he rejects both Eutyches and Nestorius but is closest to the Nestorian position in speaking about the two natures of Christ, as if each was an active subject alongside the other. "Each of the natures performed, in solidarity with the other, those activities that were peculiar to it."[16] An Antiochene would not have expressed it so unprotected at this stage of the debate! What rescues Leo's letter is its somewhat simple and (in the eyes of an Easterner) non-reflective use of language, so that the theological formulas appear awkward rather than heretical.

When the Council of Chalcedon convened, the affair with Eutyches was fresh, and Leo's Tome lay before the council as an item of business. The Alexandrian tradition had become scandalized on account of Dioscorus' outrageous conduct during the "Robber Synod." The emperor did nothing to hide his antipathy toward Eutyches and the "Monophysites" (the radical, one-nature theologians). It seemed to be a council weighted in favor of the West and the Antiochene tradition, and the Council of Chalcedon has often been interpreted as such. Adolph Harnack has contended that the Church of the East simply was deprived of its faith by this council.[17]

New analysis of the conciliar decrees and their models point in another direction. True, a sentence from Leo's Tome can be found in the council's decrees, and the Chalcedonian confession employs the term *nature* in a manner different from what Cyril normally does. But in the Chalcedonian confession, the use of the term *nature* undoubtedly lies closer to the Antiochenes and, as already mentioned, has as its direct predecessor Flavian's usage from three years earlier. Aside from this, much of Cyril is also to be found in the council's confession, as has been highlighted in more recent scholarship.[18] Cyril could also use *nature* in other ways than the characteristic "one-nature" formula; and in its emphasis on Christ as one hypostasis, the confession was susceptible to a Cyrillian interpretation.

But, looking closer at the text, the Chalcedonian confession came about after strong imperial pressure; the bishops had long resisted every suggestion to draw up a new creedal statement. They referred to Nicea (325) and Constantinople (381) and insisted that everything that could be said had already been stated by the decrees of those two councils. But in the end, they allowed themselves to be persuaded to form a twenty-three member committee responsible for developing a creedal statement. In addition to Leo's *Tome,* the committee had Cyril's two letters against Nestorius and the union confession of 433 as its basic documents, as well as Flavian's creedal confession. This quite extensive foundational material was to be sewn together into a confessional document that was to be subscribed by all. As later history has revealed, that was a hopeless task. (Evaluations of the document have varied greatly, both then and later, not least among modern scholars.) The famous document reads as follows:

> Following, then, the holy Fathers, we all with one voice teach that it should be confessed that our Lord Jesus Christ is one and the same Son, the Same perfect in Godhead, the Same perfect in manhood, truly God and truly man, the Same [consisting] of a rational soul and a body;
>
> *homoousios* [consubstantial] with the Father as to His Godhead, and the Same *homoousios* with us as to His manhood; in all things like us, sin only excepted; begotten of the Father before ages as to His Godhead, and in the last days, for us and for our salvation, of Mary the Virgin, *theotokos,* as to His manhood;
>
> [We confess] One and the same Christ, Son, Lord, only begotten, made known in two natures [which exist] without confusion, without change, without division, without separation; the difference of the natures having been in no wise taken away by reason of the union, but rather the properties of each being preserved, and [both] concurring into one Person (*prosopon*) and one *hypostasis,* not parted or divided into two persons (*prosopa*), but one and the same Son and Only-begotten, the divine Logos, the Lord Jesus Christ; even as prophets from of old [have spoken] concerning Him, and as the Lord Jesus Christ Himself has taught us, and as the Symbol of the Fathers has delivered to us.[19]

As mentioned above, the evaluation of this confession has varied greatly. For many of Cyril's disciples, it must have been difficult to reconcile themselves to the realization that Cyril's dynamic concept of nature had been lost. It is little wonder that Chalcedon marked the beginning of that process which led many supporters of Cyril into outright church schism and the establishing of their own Monophysite churches, especially in and around Alexandria and in Syria. A number of these churches exist to this very day. If one looks at modern histories of dogma, almost always those who are enamored by Cyril's dynamic "unichristology" have a difficult time working up enthusiasm for the Chalcedonian Definition.[20]

But the confession can be viewed otherwise. One can just as well interpret it as an attempt to hold on to the best in Cyril's Christology independent of the specific Alexandrian concept of *nature* which experientially was open toward the direction of Apollinarianism and Monophysitism. The confession can be seen as an expression of simple, Biblical concepts that are used primarily to point to the active, suffering subject in Christ: *the one and same Son, our Lord Jesus Christ*; *the one and same Christ*; *the one and same Son and only begotten*. Recall that the whole Chalcedonian Definition is intended as a clarification of one single point in the Nicene Creed, namely, what it says about the incarnation. Chalcedon underscores that it is the one and same Jesus Christ who before all time was begotten of the Father and who in the latter times was born as a human being. So that no one should think that this was just an evasion (*a la* Nestorius' famous "bearer of Christ" [*Christotokos*]), the much debated "bearer of God" [theotokos] is confessed and personhood is stressed along the lines advocated by the Cappadocians: *one hypostasis*. The term *nature* is also employed in a manner similar to Flavian, in juxtaposition with the concept of a double *homoousia*. It is not the typical Cyrillian usage, but neither is it irreconcilable with the cause Cyril sought to advance. The confession was open to a Cyrillian interpretation, and so it was used later on by the so-called *Neo-Chalcedonians*. But on the other hand, the confession did not exclude the moderate Antiochenes. I personally view the Chalcedonian Definition as reflecting great theological and ecclesiological wisdom. By avoiding the Cyrillian concept of nature and at the same time formulating it in such a manner that the *issue* could be maintained, it became a necessary reminder for zealous disciples of Cyril that his use of language was neither sacrosanct, canonical, or indispensable. It hardly was the intention of the council fathers to introduce *hypostasis* and *prosopon* as a sort of canonical alternative; they merely wanted to express themselves in an unmistakable manner so that a Nestorian interpretation of the confession was impossible. That was the way the Chalcedonian Definition was clearly understood in the course of the ecclesiastical reception which followed the council.

"To Understand As Fisher Folk Do"

We are in a somewhat unique and rare position because we possess the returns of an imperial poll indicating how the confession was received and understood around the church and whether there was need for further revision. During the years 457–59 thirty-four answers were received signed by approximately 280 bishops and monks.[21] The responses reveal very clearly that the bishops did not consider the Chalcedonian Definition's use of language ("one hypostasis in two natures") as decisive. One of the bishops said that one ought to read it as a fisher would and not as Aristotle. Judging by the general response that was formulated, the council really only wanted to clarify the Nicene Creed with regard to some newly arisen false doctrine. Some of the bishops openly confess that the language of the church council is somewhat foreign to them, but they acknowledge the intent of the statement.

Grillmeier states, "It is not the terms (*hypostasis, nature*) that are significant, but the baptismal confession and baptismal instruction—in other words, the faith into which one is baptized. So strong is this contention that some of the bishops want it known that the Chalcedonian Definition can not form the basis for baptismal instruction even if they acknowledge the content of the council's decisions. . . . The usual claim that the church at Chalcedon surrendered to Hellenistic formulas and abstract theology just is not valid. In any case, that was not the self-understanding or intention of the college of bishops at that time."[22]

Only four or five bishops betray any reservations at all about the new language in the council's confession. One of them is Basileus, metropolitan of Antioch, who gives us a good example of a moderate Antiochene reading of Chalcedon. But most of the replies that contain free renderings of the confession endearingly use the distinctive *one* expressions: "one and the same. . . ." And the double *homoousia* terminology also elicits sympathy and acceptance. Regarding the two natures, one of the bishops states that Pope Leo's manner of expressing himself can no doubt cause offense for individual believers and that he could have expressed himself more clearly; but as directed against heresy, the pope's statement is quite in order—besides, it is inconsequential whether one says "unconfused unity of two natures" or simply "of two natures." Epiphanius of Perge states that even if one says "the Logos' one nature" (concerning the *fleshly incarnated* Logos!), it is all the same "but only stated in a more elegant manner"!

Practically all the responses leave a strong impression that the council desired nothing but to undergird the Nicene Creed. The meaning of the confession was first and foremost to underscore the oneness of subject in the Nicene confession: One and the same [person], who was with the Father from eternity, suffered and died.

Without doubt, the opposition was viewed as coming from two quarters, partly from those who divided the incarnated One in two, thereby losing the unity of the subject, and partly from those like Eutyches who denied His true humanity, His *homoousios* with us.

If one looks for the occasion that necessitated the council, it is certainly the Son's *homoousios* with us that is the main message of the Council of Chalcedon. In 431 the Ephesus council had stated what was needed against Nestorius. Now it was Eutyches' denial of the Son's full *homoousios* with us that had to be countered with a clear statement regarding Jesus' true and complete humanity.

We today can acquire a misleading impression when we read about the doctrinal controversies of the Early Church and think that they were over mere quibbles and hair-splitting formulas.[23] Clearly, the participants at Chalcedon did not share this view. The historical context of the document shows a conspicuous lack of quibbling, both philosophically and terminologically. The council was open to a positive assessment from the moderate, center-oriented versions of the two chief Christological traditions that were operative at the time and gave an unmistakable *no* to the tangents and one-sidedness of both extremes.

After Chalcedon

Many histories of the development of Christology end with the Council of Chalcedon. The impression is thereby given that Chalcedon marks a sort of closure, the "last word" about Christ in the Early Church's theological development. That certainly was not the case. One could rather say just the opposite: Chalcedon *opened up* the greatest Christological struggle in the Eastern church. Just as the Arian controversy became more intense after the Council of Nicea, the same happened after Chalcedon as "one nature" and "two nature" theologians opposed each other. Like the situation after Nicea, imperial ecclesiastical politics played a major role in the on-going controversy. But, unlike the controversy surrounding the Nicene Creed, the lack of unanimity regarding the Chalcedonian Definition led to permanent church schism in the Eastern church, obviously for many reasons. Ecclesiastical politics and imperial interference are certainly among them.

For political reasons, the emperor in the East was long committed to maintaining good relations with the pope in Rome after the collapse of the Western empire (finally and permanently in 476). When the emperor demanded continued allegiance to Chalcedon, the council and its confession became closely tied as well to Pope Leo's *Tome*. The pope in Rome guarded it jealously so that not a jot or a tittle of the recognition which Leo's *Tome* had received at Chalcedon would be lost. However, many, very many, in the East had problems permitting Leo's *Tome* to function as the hermeneutical principle for understanding the Chalcedon confession; these included especially the zealous adherents of Cyril's dynamic monochristology which they viewed as the only legitimate way of interpreting the Nicene Creed. That this became so distorted is directly related to what some might consider purely theological happenstance. During the period directly after Chalcedon, there were no theologians who could interpret the theological concerns of the Chalcedonian Definition so that the deep-seated incarnation beliefs of the vast majority of Eastern Christians would be recognized. And while the adherents of Cyril could muster the most gifted theologians, they were critical of Chalcedon.

The Cappadocians saw the Nicene Creed through to a theological victory, but Chalcedon acquired its "Cappadocians" [its supporters] too late. Reference is usually made to theological *Neo-Chalcedonianism* in the sixth century when theologians appeared who interpreted Chalcedon as a precise expression for the incarnated Christ's dynamic *unity* of the divine and human in a living, active person. The possibility for a common understanding with the Monophysites (Cyril's disciples) was all in place. But historically, it was too late. The opposition against Chalcedon among the Monophysites was too firmly established, and imperial ecclesiastical politics consistently torpedoed attempts at rapprochement.[24]

Within the Chalcedonian imperial church as well, peace was an elusive thing. In the seventh century new attempts were made to discover "something" in Christ which would be exempt from the two-nature point of view. Some found it in His energy (*energia,* from which came the designation the *Monergistic Controversy*); others found it in His will (*thelema,* from which came the designation the *Monotheletist Controversy*). Especially through the great Neo-Chalcedonian theologian, Maximus the Confessor, two-nature theology triumphed here as well. Maximus confronted Nicene Christology with the account of Jesus' prayer struggle in Gethsemane. He showed that, to be in harmony with the gospels' picture of Jesus, one must posit *a true human will* in Jesus, a human will that through struggle and obedience bows to the divine will.[25]

During the eighth and ninth centuries, the Christological struggles were fanned anew in the *Iconoclastic Controversy* (*eikon,* picture). Three dimensional art (sculpture) had never been allowed in the Eastern church, but pictures painted on wood panels had become very popular, especially within monasticism. These paintings, particularly those of Christ, had become more than just a pedagogical tool. In the attempt to render a faithful depiction of the Son of God, they envisioned a divine portrayal of the subject matter and the created order similar to that expressed by Cyrillian Christology. To consider it impossible to render a faithful picture of God or God's Son was to say in effect that the divine and the created order could never be united and that the incarnation was merely a blending of the two elements. Did that not say that the divine and the human in Christ only appeared to have been united? Did that not endorse Nestorius' bifurcated Christology? Understandably, against this background the Eastern church perceived its Christology to be endangered by the Iconoclastic Controversy. Its great theological theoretician, John of Damascus, who died in 749, defended the use of icons as objects of *reverence* (as opposed to *worship,* which God alone deserved) and wrote the classical summation of Eastern theology.

In conclusion, enough has been said to show that Chalcedon can just as well be considered the prelude to a new phase in the Christological controversy as the conclusion of an earlier one. Why then such great emphasis on Chalcedon? From the perspective of the Eastern church, the natural response is that Chalcedon was the catalyst for a schism in the church and that the Chalcedonian Definition has generally given the remaining portion of the orthodox church in the [Byzantine] empire its doctrinal identity. From the perspective of the Western church, it is only natural to point to the simple fact that the Chalcedonian Definition was absorbed into one of the ecumenical creeds by the West, the *Athanasian Creed,* a document, which from all indications, originated in southern France [Gaul] around the year 500 and has been adopted by most Western Christian communions. Lutherans subscribe to it as one of their confessional writings. This so-called Athanasian Creed is an echo of the Chalcedonian Definition when it states

> He is God, begotten before all worlds from the being of the Father, and He is man, born in the world from the being of His mother—existing fully as God, and fully as man with a rational soul and a human body. . . . Although He is God and man, He is not divided, but is one Christ. He is united because God has taken humanity into Himself; He does not transform deity into humanity. He is completely one in the unity of His person, without confusing His natures.[26]

Postscript: The Existential Significance of the Incarnation

The world picture of the New Testament is a mythical world picture.... The presentation of the salvation occurrence, which constitutes the real content of the New Testament proclamation, corresponds to this mythical world picture. The proclamation speaks in mythical language: the last days are at hand; "when the time had fully come," God sent His Son. The Son, a preexistent divine being, appears on earth as a man; His death on the cross, which He suffers as a sinner, makes atonement for the sins of men. His resurrection is the beginning of the cosmic catastrophe through which the death brought into the world by Adam is annihilated; the demonic powers of the world have lost their power. The risen one has been exalted to heaven at the right hand of God; He has been made "Lord" and "King." He will return on the clouds of heaven in order to complete the work of salvation; then will take place the resurrection of the dead and the last judgment; finally, sin, death, and all suffering will be done away.... *All of this is mythological talk,* and the individual motifs may be easily traced to the contemporary mythology of Jewish apocalypticism and the Gnostic myth of redemption. Insofar as it is mythological talk, *it is incredible to men and women today* because for them the mythical world picture is a thing of the past. [Italics added and are not in the original quotation]

[Jesus'] person is viewed in the light of mythology when He is said to have been begotten of the Holy Spirit and born of a virgin, and this becomes clearer still in Hellenistic Christian communities where He is understood to be the Son of God in a metaphysical sense, a great, pre-existent heavenly being who became man for the sake of our redemption and took on Himself

129

suffering, even the suffering of the cross. It is evident that such conceptions are mythological, for they were widespread in the mythologies of Jews and Gentiles and then were transferred to the historical person of Jesus. Particularly the conception of the pre-existent Son of God who descended in human guise into the world to redeem mankind is part of the Gnostic doctrine of redemption, and nobody hesitates to call this doctrine mythological. This raises in an acute form the question, *What is the importance of the preaching of Jesus and of the preaching of the New Testament as a whole for modern man?* [Italics in the original quotation].[1]

Both of the above quotations are from Rudolf Bultmann. I can still remember the deep unrest that gripped me when, as a young theological student, I first read these lines. It seemed to me that the problem to which Bultmann pointed was a real problem. I did not reflect at that time upon the interesting fact that when Bultmann seeks to summarize the message of the mythological Christ in the New Testament, his account sounds exactly like a free rendering of the Nicene Creed. But if I had at that time reflected about it, I would no doubt have said, "So much the worse, because it reveals that there actually is a mythological framework in the New Testament that has taken center place in the Early Church's confession of Christ. If it actually is true that one can easily demonstrate the most striking mythological parallels to virtually every statement of the creed (with the exception of 'suffered under Pontius Pilate, was crucified, died and was buried'), then the situation must no doubt be quite critical."

[Bultmann is not the only theologian to explore the topic of myth and the incarnation.] In 1977 a group of English theologians published *The Myth of God Incarnate*.[2] It aroused considerable debate because a group of influential theologians in the Anglican Church raised a challenge that seemed similar to Bultmann's.[3] But on several points they departed radically from Bultmann. It seems natural to point them out as we draw [this volume] to a close. While Bultmann does not have the slightest misgiving about the religious-historical background for the concept of the incarnation, the English authors are groping and searching that issue. They express themselves with much more reservation than Bultmann. Quite clearly, none of the authors is willing to endorse Bultmann's view that the

the idea of incarnation is all very easily derived from Gnostic myths of redemption. Few scholarly positions have had to endure such treatment in recent research as has this Bultmann myth,[4] which has disintegrated and virtually disappeared from debate. If any relatively certain conclusion can be drawn from the last few decades of research regarding the background of New Testament Christology, it is the acknowledgment that handy, available myths, with the same structure as the confession of Christ that could easily be transferred to Jesus, just are not to be found, in spite of the fact that many have searched for them. With much more confidence it can be said that the building blocks in the doctrine of the incarnation are *Jewish*. Belief in the incarnation arose among Jews who considered it from Jewish presuppositions.

We return to the paradox described at the beginning of this book: the doctrine of the incarnation arose in a religious environment which for the most part would have been thought to exclude such a possibility. In Hellenistic religion, the boundaries between the divine, the human, and the world were somewhat fluid. While in actual fact the gods could not become human beings, the common view was that certain select human beings could cross the boundary into the divine sphere and be elevated as gods. In a world of thought where the boundaries between the divine and the human were unclear, it might seem that conditions were ripe for something that could *be likened* to the Christian doctrine of the incarnation. But this belief arose among people who drew the sharpest possible line of separation between God and creation and for whom every attempt to erase this distinction was blasphemy. Looking at the further development of the doctrine of the incarnation, we note particularly that those who shaped the doctrine were thoroughly schooled in a philosophical tradition whose starting point was very anti-mythological and who understood the word *theology* (coined by Plato) as a slogan highly critical of myth. They believed that myth had to be laid aside, for only via the intellect can one arrive at a satisfactory concept of deity.[5] The doctrine of the incarnation was formulated by theologians for whom the Old Testament passages ascribing human attributes to God were very offensive! The great theologians of the third and fourth centuries would have contended that Bultmann was inexcusably naive when he imagined that *up* and *down* in the New Testament and the language of the creeds meant that the eternal God allowed Himself to be localized in a physical sense to a place *up there*. They taught that God was not only beyond the created world but also beyond all our comprehension and conception. *These* were the theologians who clung to and expanded upon the doctrine of the incarnation!

Could not the doctrine of Christ be explained as having arisen out of a "primitive" setting such as would have had to exist at the outset of the history of the doctrine, a setting in which there existed a "mythological pressure" in the direction of a doctrine of the incarnation?

We have outlined the following simple, historical scenario: Judaism knew many messiah-candidates, wonder-workers, charismatic scribes, great exorcists, both before and after Jesus. But never was anything said regarding them that came close to what the early wisdom Christology said about Jesus.[6] The cultural environment was the same. The religious, historical presuppositions were the same for all of them. But what was asserted regarding Jesus was unique. Thus the explanation can not be found in the cultural environment; it must be found in an entirely different place—with Jesus Himself. What is said about Jesus is so different because Jesus *was* so different and because what happened to Him was so different. To me, many New Testament scholars reveal a woeful lack of historical insight when they question whether the primitive church's Christology has any relationship to Jesus Himself. Of course, it has! Otherwise it becomes completely unexplainable.

We will not review what we developed in the second chapter regarding wisdom Christology's significance in the disciples' experience of Jesus' unique authority even before the Easter event. When John relates that Thomas the Twin fell down before the resurrected Jesus and exclaimed "My Lord and my God!" the evangelist undoubtedly means that this acknowledgment had first dawned for the disciples as a suspicion or question of the disciples but could be stated directly and without reservation only after the meeting with the risen One. I believe the evangelist is painting an historical picture when he presents the material in this manner, for this gives meaning and sense to what happens afterwards. That such a confession could later be questioned and agonized over, and in Hebrew Christian communities like the Ebionites be directly opposed and replaced by a Jewish "orthodox" messianism—that can be easily understood. But I have great difficulty imagining that the idea of incarnation could start with an Ebionite-Adoptionist Christology, then gradually and almost imperceptibly (and without powerful echoes of protest!) evolve into a Christology which we meet in a John or Paul. We know, for example, that Paul's Christology could not have been viewed as anything special or remarkable either in Rome or Jerusalem. The controversy regarding Paul related to completely different questions, as the Epistle to the Romans clearly demonstrates.

In the investigation of the Early Church's incarnation-Christology as it was eventually formulated at Chalcedon, I have tried to show that behind the (for us) somewhat unfamiliar language, something quite simple was stated: Jesus' *I* is identical with that Wisdom or Logos of God, which is identical with God's own salvific and creative intention through which the world was created. At the same time, the Early Church insisted that Jesus was a completely human being; He "lacked" nothing in order to be a human being. The divine within Him had not surpressed the human or taken its place in any way whatsoever. His *I* was a true human *I*. This, expressed in Chalcedon's somewhat abstract language, stated that the natures were united but without commingling. *Without commingling* declares that Jesus' divinity and humanity are both intact, that they do not annul each other, that He is God and human in one person. That this should be thinkable for us, that our psychological intuition should be able to empathize with Jesus' own consciousness regarding the mystery of His person—that thought would no doubt have appeared outrageous to the Early Church theologians. That they in their confessional formulations should have given some sort of *explanation* regarding the "how" of the incarnation would have appeared just as far removed. What they wanted was to hold on to the mystery, which could be believed, taught, and confessed—but not explained.

I have tried to imagine the Nicene fathers in dialog with a modern New Testament scholar who finds it safest and psychologically most reasonable to place Jesus in a *representative* category of one sort or another—such as the final, eschatological prophet or something similar. I think the fathers would say that Jesus appears only—not even primarily—as God's or Wisdom's representative. He bursts all representative categories through His own *I,* this divine author-

133

itative *I* which we meet throughout the gospels, in the most dissimilar stories. He does not speak as a *representative* would speak. A representative speaks in the name of the person who has sent him. But Jesus speaks in His own name. His utterance gives meaning only if His *I* is that of Wisdom's, and thereby in a certain sense God's. When Jesus said, "Before Abraham was, I am," that was when the Jews wanted to stone Him, for they knew the significance of what He said.

The early Christians thought that, in the human being called Jesus, they had met Wisdom, the Logos, the eternal, creative thought through which God had created the world. That one, who delighted in the presence of God when the world and the human race were created, through His death and resurrection became the head of a new race that through Him partakes in the resurrection from the dead. God's creative thought, His wisdom, appeared as folly when God's Son allowed Himself to be crucified.

Faith in a Jesus who was God's incarnated Wisdom, an *I* identical with God's eternal creative thought, arose not because of "mythological pressure" in a *subsequent* cultural environment far removed from the shores of the Sea of Galilee. It arose because of a "theological pressure" which lay inherent in Jesus' own Jewish context and which became unleashed through this context's own encounter with Jesus—the *historical* Jesus.

Abbreviations

ANF: Alexander Roberts and James Donaldson, eds., *The Ante-Nicene Fathers,* vols 1–10 (Grand Rapids, 1971–78).

CCL: Corpus Christianorum, Series Latina, Turnhout, 1953ff. The first two volumes of this edition of the Latin church fathers contain the collected writings of Tertullian. *CCL* 2:1176.17–24 pertains to volume 2, page 1176, lines 17–24.

Chadwick: Henry Chadwick, *Origen: Contra Celsum, Translated with an Introduction and Notes* (Cambridge, 1965). I refer to relevant pages in this exceptional translation.

Danby: H. Danby, *The Mishnah* (Oxford, 1933). There are numerous later reprint editions.

Goodspeed: Edgar J. Goodspeed, *Die ältesten Apologeten. Texte mit kurzen Einleitungen* (Göttingen, 1914; rep. 1984). This is the most frequently used edition of Justin's writings. I refer to page and line.

Grant: Robert M. Grant, *Theophilus of Antioch: Ad Autolycum,* Oxford Early Christian Texts (Oxford, 1970). Greek text with English translation on facing pages. My citations include both text and translation.

Hall: Stuart G. Hall, *Melito of Sardis: On Pascha and Fragments,* Oxford Early Christian Texts (Oxford, 1979). Greek text with English translation on facing pages. My citations include both text and translation.

Lauterbach: J. Z. Lauterbach, *Mekilta de-Rabbi Ishmael I–III* (Philadelphia, 1933). I have used the 1976 paperback edition. Hebrew text with English translation on facing pages. Citations cover both text and tranlation.

Loeb: *The Loeb Classical Library* (Cambridge, MA, 1912–). This series contains handy editions of the original texts together with English translations on facing pages. I have referred to the editions of The Apostolic Fathers, Josephus and Philo: Kirsopp Lake, *The*

Apostolic Fathers, 2 vols.; H. S. J. Thackeray and Ralph Marcus, *Josephus,* 9 vols.; and F. H. Colson et al, *Philo,* 10 vols. Volume numbers refer to volume number of each author. Page numbers cover both text and translation.

New Eusebius: J. Stevenson, *A New Eusebius. Documents Illustrating the History of the Church to A.D. 337.* New revised edition by W. H. C. Frend (London, 1987). A handy and comprehensive English translation.

NPNF: Philip Schaff and Henry Wace, eds., *A Select Library of Nicene and Post-Nicene Fathers,* Second series, vols. 1–6. (Grand Rapids, 1952–54). Citations from this translation are from Eusebius (vol. 1) and Athanasius (vol. 4). In addition, several citations from the Arian Controversy are to be found in volume 3. Citation format is the same as in *ANF.*

OT Pseud.: James H. Charlesworth, ed., *The Old Testament Pseudepigrapha,* 2 vols. (New York, 1983–85).

Outler: Albert C. Outler, ed., *Augustine: Confessions and Enchiridion,* Library of Christian Classics 7 (Philadelphia, n.d.).

SC: Sources Chrétiennes (Paris, 1941 ff.). (*Editions du Cerf*).

Soncino: Soncino Press named after the Spanish rabbi who in the late Middle Ages made the standard Hebrew translation of the Babylonian Talmud and the Midrash Rabba. English translations are by Isidore Epstein, ed., *The Babylonian Talmud,* 34 vols. (London, 1935–48); Harry Freedman and Maurice Simon, *Midrash Rabba I-X* (3rd ed., London, 1983). Page numbers refer to these English translations.

TB: A reference to the Babylonian Talmud (*Talmud Babli*).

TU: A reference to *Texte und Untersuchungen zur Geschichte der altchristlichen Literatur.*

Urk.: A reference to *Urkunden zur Geschichte des arianischen Streites 318–328,* edited by H. G. Opitz.

Whittaker: M. Whittaker, *Tatian: Oratio ad Graecos and Fragments,* Oxford Early Christian Texts (Oxford, 1982). Greek text with English translation on facing pages. My citations cover both text and translation.

Notes

Chapter 1: The "Impossible" Dogma

1. Adolf von Harnack, *What Is Christianity?* Thomas B. Saunders, trans. (New York, 1923). [Divine pronouns are capitalized throughout this translation of Skarsaune, *Incarnation,* often for the sake of clarity. Because Adolf von Harnack was an Adoptionist, the pronouns in this instance have not been capitalized.]

2. Abu Yusuf Ya'qub al-Qirqisani was *karait,* that is, a follower of a Jewish movement which did not recognize the rabbis' oral law tradition. In A.D. 937 he wrote *The Book About the Light and the Watchtower* (Kitab al-Anwar wal-Maraqib), in which he describes and criticizes rabbinic, Christian, and Muslim syntax. His description of the origin of Christianity and his critique of Christian doctrine appear strikingly modern. See the translation of relevant sections in Leon Nemoy, "Al-Qirqisani's Account of the Jewish Sects and Christianity," *Hebrew Union College Annual* 7 (1930), 317–97, especially 364ff. Cf. also Daniel J. Lasker, *Jewish Philosophical Polemics Against Christianity in the Middle Ages* (New York, 1977), 57–60.

3. "A Jewish View of Jesus," a transcript from an interview on Norwegian television April 24, 1977, and reproduced in *Jøder og kristne. Bidrag til en dialog* (Oslo, 1978), 82–99. Quotation is from pp. 94f.

4. From the large body of literature note one of the "classics," Wilhelm Bousset's *Kyrios Christos. Geschichte des Christusglaubens von den Anfängen bis Irenäus,* 3d ed. (Göttingen, 1926).

5. Regarding the ancient concept of God and the doctrine of God's immutability, see Werner Elert, *Der Ausgang der altkirchlichen Christologie* (Berlin, 1957), 74–132; Wolfgang Pannenberg, "Die Aufnahme des philosophischen Gottesbegriffs als dogmatisches Problem der frühchristlichen Theologie," *Zeitschrift für Kirchengeschichte* 70 (1959), 1–45; republished by Pannenberg in *Grundfragen systematischer Theologie, Gesammelte Aufsätze,* 2d ed. (Göttingen, 1971), 296–345; as well as Robert M. Grant, *The Early Christian Doctrine of God* (Charlottesville, 1966), esp. 111–14; and G. L. Prestige, *God in Patristic Thought,* 2d ed. (London, 1952, paperback ed. 1964), 6–9. Cf. also my article "Gudsbildet i Oldkirkens teologi," *Tidsskrift for teologi og kirke* 48 (1977), 179–92.

6. *CCL* 2:1176.17–24; *ANF* 3:609.1.

7. *CCL* 2:1181.24–32; *ANF* 3:612.1.

8. *CCL* 2:506.26–30; *ANF* 3:319.1.

9. " ... *et haec nec de Filio Dei credenda fuissent si scripta non essent, fortasse non credenda de Patre, licet scripta ....*" *CCL* 2:1182.51f; *ANF* 3:612.2.

137

10. Quoted from Origen's polemic against Celsus, *Contra Celsum* 4.14 (*SC* 136:216.4–12; Chadwick, 192f).

11. *Contra Celsum* 4.18 (*SC* 136.224.4–7; Chadwick, 195).

12. *Contra Celsum* 5.2 (*SC* 147.16.2f; Chadwick, 264).

13. Cf., e.g., *Contra Celsum* 6.42–47,78; 1.67. Also with the Christian apologist, Tatian (a contemporary of Celsus), one finds clear evidence that Christians are blamed for misunderstanding the myths because they take them all too literally: *Oratio* chap. 21 (Whittaker, 42–45).

14. Augustine, *Confessions* 7.9 (Outler, 144–46).

15. *ANF* 1:227.1 (Goodspeed, 165.9–12).

16. *De Carne Christi* 6.1, 4; (*CCL* 1:800.2–9; 881:26–29; *ANF* 3:525.1–2). The latter part of the quotation is often shortened to *credo quia absurdum,* causing the misunderstanding that Tertullian was an early anti-rationalist. That he was not. His argument is quite rational. The unbelievableness of the Christian doctrine of the incarnation reveals that it has not been not thought through [double negative is intentional] and in other words must be true: *crucifixus est dei filius; non pudet, quia pudendum est. Et mortuus est dei filius; credibile est, quia ineptum est. Et sepultus surrexit; certum est, quia impossibile.*

17. As a representative and instructive example of this new trend, I point to James D. G. Dunn, *Christology in the Making. A New Testament Inquiry Into the Origin of the Doctrine of the Incarnation* (Philadelphia, 1980).

Chapter 2: The Incarnation in the New Testament

1. *ANF* 1:219.2; Goodspeed 147:6–13.

2 The closest the rabbis seem to have come to any thoughts about preexistence is the declaration about the Messiah's *name* being created before the rest of creation together with six other works of creation: "Seven things were created before the creation of the world: the Torah, repentance, Eden's hedge, Gehenna, the Throne of Glory, Holiness, and the Messiah's name" (*TB, Pes.* 54a; Soncino, 265). Scriptural grounds for the preexistence of the Messiah's name in relationship to the other works of creation is found in Ps. 72:17. *Genesis Rabba* (no doubt after the Talmudic era) emphasizes that there is no reference to a real preexistence: "Six things (were created) before the creation of the world; some of them were really created and some others (only) in God's thought to be created later. The Torah and the Throne of Glory were really created, . . . the Messiah's name arose in God's thought to be created later" (*Gen. Rab.* 1.4; Soncino trans. 6). It is possible that this assertion was employed against the Christian attempt to use Ps. 72:17 as a prooftext for the Messiah's personal preexistence as we find it in Justin (*Dialogue* 45.4; 76.7; Irenaeus, *Demonstration* 43; etc.). Cf. the question of the Messiah's preexistence in Judaism in Hermann L. Strack and Paul Billerbeck, *Kommentar zum Neuen Testament aus Talmud und Midrash* (Munich, 1922–61), 2:333–352. I believe Billerbeck's conclusion is correct: Jewish literature is acquainted with three forms of the Messiah's "preexistence": "a. seine ideelle Präexistenz in der Gedankenwelt Gottes; b. seine virtuelle Präexistenz in seinen Ahnen . . . ; c. die reale Präexistenz seiner Seele. Keine dieser Präexistenzweisen wird dem Messias beigelegt, um ihn dadurch seinem Wesen nach über die übrigen Menschen hinaus erheben, denn

die gleiche Präexistenzweise würde im Sinne der betreffenden Autoren ja auch allen Menschen eignen" (Ibid. 352).

3. In addition to Wilhelm Bousset's classic presentation (cf. note 4 in chap. 1), I can cite a recent work with the same point of view: Gösta Lindeskog, "Messianologie und Christologie," in *Das jüdisch-christliche Problem. Randglossen zu einer Forschungsepoche* (Acta Universitatis Upsaliensis, Historia Religionum 9), Uppsala, 1986, 111–44. Author is also the editor.

4. It applies especially when Wisdom is identified with the Law. Cf. below.

5. In *Targum Jerushalmi. Targum Neofoti* has the same understanding of Gen. 1:1 but translates *bereshit* twice: *mileqadim bechokmah bara* . . . . Many rabbinic references to the same combination of Gen. 1:1 and Prov. 8:22 are cited in Billerbeck 2:356f. Cf. also the interesting analysis in K. Schubert, "Einige Beobachtungen zum Verständnis des Logosbegriffes im Frührabbinischen Schrifttum," *Judaica* 9 (1953), 65–80.

6. In Aquila's translation: *eteken,* something that gives a perfect terminological basis for the word *protótokos* in the Epistle to the Colossians.

7. In an interesting, detailed study of the concept *arché,* C. F. Burney states that in the material found in Col. 1:15ff, there is a typical Midrashic exegesis of *bereshit* ("in the beginning") in Gen. 1:1. *Bereshit* is explained in verse 16 as *en autô, di autou* and *eis auton; reshit* as *kefalê, archê* (verse 18) and *protótokos* (verse 15). Cf. "Christ as the APXH of Creation (Prov VII 22, Col I 15–18, Rev III 14)," *Journal of Theological Studies* 27 (1926), 160–77.

8. This sentence is regarded by many as a Christian interpolation. In that case, it is completely possible that it shows that Christian copyists early recognized this passage to be a "Christological text." Cf. discussion in G. Schimanowski, *Weisheit und Messias* (Wissenschaftliche Untersuchung zum Neues Testamentum, 2:17), Tübingen, 1985, 63f.

9. In the older literature, one can mention: H. Windisch, "Die göttliche Weisheit der Juden und die paulinische Christologie," in A. Deissmann and H. Windisch, eds., *Neutestamentliche Studien Georg Heinrici* (Leipzig, 1914), 220–34. A representative of the latest scholarly position is E. Larsson, "Kristus och skapelsen i nytestamentligt hymnmaterial," in *Deus Creator. Bidrag til skapelsesteologien* (Festskrift for Ivar P. Seierstad, Oslo, 1971), 69–84; R.E. Brown, *The Gospel According to John (i-xii)* (New York, 1966), 521–23; R. G. Hamerton–Kelly, *Pre-Existence, Wisdom, and The Son of Man. A Study of the Idea of Pre-Existence in The New Testament.* Society for New Testament Studies, Monograph Series 21 (Cambridge, 1973); J. D. G. Dunn, *Christology in the Making* (cf. note 17 in chap. 1 above), 163–250; and R. H. Fuller and P. Perkins, *Who Is This Christ? Gospel Christology and Contemporary Faith* (Philadelphia, 1983), 53–66.

10. A broader and comprehensive treatment of this theme is in the Danish edition of this book: *Inkarnationen . . . ,* 24–29.

11. Regarding the concept of wisdom in the Old Testament and Judaism, see among others: W. Schencke, *Die Chokma (Sophia) in der jüdischen Hypostasenspekulation* (Skrifter utgitt av Det Norske Videnskapsakademi 2, 1912 no.6), Kristiania, 1913; H. Ringgren, *Word and Wisdom. Studies in the Hypostatization of Divine Qualities and Functions in the Ancient Near East* (Lund, 1947); B. L. Mack, *Logos und Sophia. Untersuchungen zur Weisheitstheologie im hellenistischen Judentum.* Studien zur Umwelt des Neuen Testaments 10 (Göttingen,

1973); M. Kuchler, *Frühjüdische Weisheitstraditionen. Zum Fortgang weisheit-lichen Denkens im Bereich des frühjüdischen Jahweglaubens.* Orbis biblicus et orientalis 26 (Freiburg, 1979).

12. For the confrontation between Judaism and Hellenic culture, see especially M. Hengel, *Judaism and Hellenism*, 2 vols. (Philadelphia, 1974). One will benefit greatly from reading the books of Elias Bickermann. He holds many of Hengel's points of view: *The God of the Maccabees*, Studies in the Judaism of Late Antiquity 32 (Leiden, 1979); *From Ezra to the Last of the Maccabees* (New York, 1962).

13. Cf. parallel wisdom section in Baruch 3f (cited above): "She [Wisdom] is the book of the commandments of God, and the law that endures for ever" (Bar. 4:1).

14. An obvious allusion to Ex. 13:21f: "The Lord went before them by day in a pillar of cloud to lead them along the way, and by night in a pillar of fire to give them light. . . ." Indirectly the author identifies Wisdom with God when He appears on earth.

15. This explains how Wisdom could become such a dominant concept within all sections of Judaism during the last few centuries before Christ. M. Küchler describes the Jewish "conceptualization process" [*sapientalisering*] as follows: "Einmal zeigte sich, dass der Anspruch auf Weisheitsbesitz ein Charakteristikum *aller* frühjüdischen Bekenntningsgruppen war. Der Weise ist eine allgegen-wärtige Gestalt. Die weisheitliche Terminologie geht quer durch alle Schul- und Meinungsrichtungen. Der Anspruch auf die entscheidende Weisheit wird sowohl von den angesehenen *soferim* von Gesetz und Sitte als auch von den apokalyptischen *hasidim* aller Schattierungen—eingeschlossen die Extremisten in Qumran und die Jesuaner in Galiläa und Jerusalem—sowohl von den phar-isäischen Schulen Hillels und Schammais als auch von den christlichen Theo-logen und Predigern erhoben. Mit Recht kann man deshalb von einem 'sapientalen Milieu' sprechen, von einem Klima des Eros nach *da'at/gnôsis,* in welchem sich die juüdische Gruppenbildung vollzog" (*Frühjüdische Weis-heitstraditionen,* 15).

16. An interesting analysis of soteriology in The Wisdom of Solomon is found in B. L. Mack, *Logos und Sophia* (see note 11), 79–95.

17. It is still striking that Moses has 10 verses in chapter 45 while Aaron receives 30!

18. Gerhard von Rad has rightly insisted in *Weisheit in Israel* (Neukirchen-Vluyn, 1970), 314ff, that Wisdom, not Law, is the dominant concept in Ecclesiasticus.

19. *Genesis Rabba,* 1.1 (Soncino trans. 1). This thought about the Torah as the primeval image is further expanded upon in Jewish mystical thinking. In *Sefer Yetzirah* it is stated that the 22 letters with which the Law was written and the ten *Sefiroth* which emanate from God, represent the ideal material and shape with which the world was made. "Stripped of all its symbolism and mystical formulations, the underlying philosophy of the Sefer Yetzirah is the celebrated Theory of Ideas" (I. Epstein, *Judaism. A Historical Presentation.* Baltimore, 1968. 228).

20. *Moreh Nabukhim* (Guide to the Perplexed 2.6) is here cited according to E. E. Urbach, *The Sages—Their Concepts and Beliefs,* vol. 1 (Jerusalem, 1975),

199. Also in this is a commentary on the Midrash with a comparison by Philo of corresponding parables, *De Opificio Mundi,* 17–20.

21. Marcus Ehrenpreis, *Talmud, Fariseism, Urkristendom* (1933); cited here according to E. Thestrup Pedersen, *Jesu forkyndelse,* 4th ed. (Copenhagen, 1980), 107f.

22. "The Rabbi as Word Made Flesh"; J. Neusner, *Midrash in Context. Exegesis in Formative Judaism* (Philadelphia, 1983), 136f.

23. Geza Vermes, *Jesus the Jew. A Historian's Reading of the Gospels* (London, 1973).

24. Ibid., 69–80.

25. *Misjna Taanit* 3.8 (Danby, 198).

26. Concerning Solomon as the great exorcist, see page 41.

27. Here, as so often elsewhere, it is very difficult to devise a simple evolutionary hypothesis, i.e., that the "simple" or "primitive" Christology of necessity is older and earlier than "high-Christology." Cf. the general critique of this position in C. F. D. Moule, *The Origin of Christology* (Cambridge, 1977).

28. What about the Messiah? Could the role of Messiah explain Jesus' unique power and authority? Not by itself. The role of Messiah was also a representative one. The Messiah has no divine "I" in the contemporary Jewish literature around the time of Jesus.

29. See for example the material that has been collected and published by L. Ginzberg, *The Legends of the Jews,* (Philadelphia, 1968), 4:149–154; 6:291–93; K. Preisendanz, "Solomon," in August F. Pauly, ed., *Realenzyklopaedie der classischen Altertumswissenschaft,* Supp. Vol. 8 (Stuttgart, 1956), 660–704.

30. E.g., *Misjna Aboth* 3.5 (Danby, 450): "God takes the Roman yoke and the earthly worries away from those who take upon themselves the Law's yoke." The words are attributed to Rabbi Nechonja ben Ha-qana (ca. A.D. 70). Cf. Hermann L. Strack and Paul Billerbeck, *Kommentar zum Neuen Testament aus Talmud und Midrash* (Munich, 1922–61), 1:608.

31. Note especially Sverre Aalen's article "Visdomsforestillingen og Jesu kristologiske selvbevissthet," in *Svensk exegetisk Årbok* 37/38 (1972/73), 35ff; reprinted in S. Aalen, *Guds Sønn og Guds rike. Nytestamentlige studier* (Oslo, 1973), 313–24. Wisdom-Christology redaction criticism in the Synoptics: F. Christ, *Jesus Sophia. Die Sophia-Christologie bei den Synoptikern.* Arbeiten zur Theologie des Alten und Neuen Testaments 57 (Zurich, 1970); J.M. Suggs, *Wisdom, Christology and Law in Matthew's Gospel* (Cambridge, 1970); D.W. Smith, *Wisdom Christology in the Synoptic Gospels* (Rome, 1970); Dunn, *Christology in the Making,* 196–206. Regarding the question whether this wisdom Christology is self-limiting to a redaction pattern in the synoptic gospels, see Aalen's article and my notes in *Inkarnationen* [Danish ed.], 30–32.

32. Gottfried Schimanowski, *Weisheit und Messias* in *Wissenschaftliche Untersuchung zum Neuen Testament,* 2:17 (Tübingen, 1985). My work has been written independently of Schimanowski's study. I find it interesting that he also uses the Ethiopic Book of Enoch's illustrations as the most important source for a messianology which combines *Messiah* and *Wisdom*; see *Weisheit,* 153–206.

33. Cf. P. Volz, *Die Eschatologie der jüdischen Gemeinde im neutestamentlichen Zeitalter* (Tübingen, 1934), 173ff.

34. Cf., e.g., Sh. Talmon's interesting study "Typen der Messiaserwartung um die Zeitwende," *Probleme biblischer Theologie, Gerhard von Rad zum 70. Geburtstag,* H. W. Wolff, ed. (Munich, 1971), 571–88.

35. Correctly propounded by J. Neusner, *The Rabbinic Traditions about the Pharisees before 70* (Leiden, 1971), 3 vols.

36. On the other hand, it does not seem that "son of man" was used as a title but rather as a description of the visionary appearing figure in Dan. 7:13: "one which appeared (looked like) a human being." It is therefore not likely that "Son of Man" as a self-description from Jesus' own mouth is dependent on the illustrations or the tradition behind them. See especially R. Leivestad, "Der apokalyptische Menschensohn ein theologisches Phantom," *Annual of the Swedish Theological Institute* 6 (1968), 49–105; R. Leivestad, "Er den apokalyptiske menneskesønn en moderne teologisk oppfinnelse?" *Norsk teologisk tidsskrift* 70 (1969), 221–35; G. Vermes, *Jesus the Jew,* Fontana paperback ed. (London, 1976), 173–76; M. Muller, *Der Ausdruck 'Menschensohn' in den Evangelien. Voraussetzungen und Bedeutung,* Acta Theologica Danica 17 (Leiden, 1984), 67–80.

37. James H. Charlesworth, ed., *The Old Testament Pseudepigrapha,* 2 vols. (Garden City, N.Y., 1983), 1:34.

38. Ibid., 1:36–7.

39. Ibid., 1:35. There appears to be here an allusion to Ps. 72:17 which the rabbis also (later?) alleged as an instance of the Messiah's name being created before the world. Cf. above, note 2.

40. Ibid.

41. Ibid., 1:38.

42. For example, the curious work, *The Testament of Solomon,* a Jewish story embellished with Christian elements borrowed from the gospels.

43. See especially L. Ginzburg, *The Legends of the Jews* 4:149–54, and the notes in 6:291–93.

44. *Antiquities* 8.45–49 (Loeb ed. 5:594–97).

45. Cf. E. Lövestam, "Jesus Fils de David chez les Synoptiques," *Studia Theologica* 28 (1974), 97–109; K. Berger, "Die königlichen Messiastraditionen des Neuen Testaments," *New Testament Studies* 20 (1974), 1–44; D. C. Duling, "Solomon, Exorcism, and the Son of David," *Harvard Theological Review* 68 (1975), 235–52.

46. Ps. 89:26f states, "He shall cry to Me, 'Thou art my Father (*abi atah*). . . . And I will make him first-born' " (*bekor,* LXX: *prototokos*). In the targum on the Psalms, the cry of David (Messiah?) reads: *abba!* Cf. J. Jeremias, *Neutestamentliche Theologie, Erster Teil: Die Verkündigung Jesu* (Gütersloh, 1971), 71; M. Hengel, *Der Sohn Gottes. Die Entstehung der Christologie und die jüdisch-hellenistische Religionsgeschichte,* 2 ed. (Tübingen, 1977), 77f, note 89: "Hier könnte die—sicher auf Jesus zurückgehende—Wurzel des Gebetsrufs 'Abba' im Urchristentum liegen."

47. Cf. O. Betz, *What Do We Know About Jesus?* (London, 1968), 87ff, 96ff; D. C. Duling, "The Promises to David and their Entrance into Christianity: Nailing down a Likely Hypothesis," *New Testament Studies* 20 (1973/74), 55–77.

48. Cf. "the Kingdom of the Lord" and David's son(s) in 1 and 2 Chronicles in

Sverre Aalen, " 'Kingdom' and 'House' in Pre-Christian Judaism," in *Guds Sønn og Guds Rike* (Oslo, 1973), 59–66; and Magne Sæbø, "Messianisme hos Kronisten?" *Israel—Kristus—Kirken*. Festskrift til Sverre Aalen (Oslo, 1979), 53–75, esp. 66–69.

49. I contend that R. Leivestad has convincingly argued that during His earthly life Jesus was conscious of being *Messias designatus* but not yet *Messias inthronisatus*. *Hvem ville Jesus være* (Oslo, 1982), 86–183; "Hvem ville Jesus være?" in S. Hidal et al., ed., *Judendom och kristendom under de första århundradena* (Stavanger, 1986), 1:112–24.

Chapter 3: Incarnation Thought during the First Two Centuries

1. E. J. Goodspeed, ed., *Die ältesten Apologeten. Texte mit kurzen Einleitungen* (Göttingen, 1914; reprint 1984), 126:4–9; *ANF* 1:201.1. This objection (Jesus did not redeem Israel and the world) has been repeated later with regular consistency in the modern religious dialogue. Examples from the Middle Ages and recent modern times are cited in my book *Da skriften ble åpnet. Den første kristne tolkning av Det gamle testamente* (Oslo, 1987), 66–70. Cf. otherwise D. Berger and M. Wyshogrod, *Jews and "Jewish Christianity"* (New York, 1978), 19ff and my article "Oldkirkens kristologi og de jødiske frelsesforventningene" in *Judendom och kristendom under de första århundradena* (Stavanger, 1986), 2:201–219.

2. It is interesting to note that the expression "hypostasis," as it is used by modern scholars, is derived from the early church's doctrine of the Trinity!

3. Cf. esp. A. M. Goldberg, *Untersuchungen über die Vorstellung von der Schekhinah in der frühen rabbinischen Literatur—Talmud und Midrasch*. Studia Judaica. Forschungen zur Wissenschaft des Judentums 5 (Berlin, 1969); P. Kuhn, *Gottes Selbsterniedrigung in der Theologie der Rabbinen*. Studien zum Alten und Neuen Testament, vol. 17 (Munich, 1968). Cf. also the shorter but enlightening discussion in Urbach, *The Sages* 1:37–65, (cf. chap. 2, note 20).

4. Cf. Strack and Billerbeck, *Kommentar* 2:302–33, as representative of the older scholarship; and R. Hayward, *Divine Name and Presence: The Memra* (Totowa, N.J., 1981) as representative of a more modern position.

5. Philo, *On Abraham*, 119–22 (Loeb ed. 6:62–65). In the parallel explanation of *Questions and Answers on Genesis* 4:2, the following statement appears as an introduction to the exegesis of Genesis 18: "For those who have the gift of discernment, Moses presents it as quite natural *for one to be three and for three to be one, for they are one by a higher principle*. When God is considered together with His two highest powers, the creative and royal, He takes on the appearance of three to the human mind" (Loeb ed. Supp. 1:270). Cf. G. Kretschmar, *Studien zur frühchristlichen Trinitätstheologie*. Beitrage zur historischen Theologie, vol. 21 (Tübingen, 1956), 86.

6. Cf. source references and discussion in G. Kretschmar, ibid., 110–13.

7. Robert M. Grant, *The Apostolic Fathers*. Vol. 4 *Ignatius of Antioch* (Camden, N.J., 1966), 63.

8. To this passage and the parallel in *Magn.* 8:2, cf. esp. B. L. Mack, *Logos und Sophia*, 102–105 (chap. 2, note 11); A. Cabaniss, "Wisdom 18, 14f.: An Early Christmas Text," *Vigiliae Christianae* 10 (1956), 97–102.

9. Here the same is said of Logos as is said in chapter 10f about Wisdom.

10. Grant, *The Apostolic Fathers*, 4:49–50.

11. Charlesworth, *Pseudepigrapha*, 1:536.

12. See esp. *Phila.* 8:2 (Loeb ed. 1:246f) where it seems that Ignatius knew the Scriptural evidence as arranged according to the message [*kerygma*] of Christ. This Christ *kerygma* seemed to function as a "hermeneutical standard" [*tolkningskanon*] for the Old Testament.

13. Grant, *Apostolic Fathers: Ignatius,* 78. One finds similar creedal outlines in *Eph. 7:12, 18:2; Smyrn. 1:1f.* Cf. J. N. D. Kelly, *Early Christian Creeds*, 3d. ed. (London, 1972), 68–70.

14. It occurs in the parallel section in *Smyrn. 1:1.* For that matter, there is reason to believe that Ignatius shares the view that soon developed in the second century that Jesus' Davidic lineage stemmed from Mary. Cf. Walter Bauer, *Das Leben Jesus im Zeitalter der neutestamentlichen Apokryphen* (Tübingen, 1909), 27ff.

15. 1 John 4:1–3, 2 John 7; the Gnostic Christology in the second century. Irenaeus already states that the Gnostics ground their docetic Christology in the idea that Christ being divine is *naturaliter impassibilis;* cf. *Against Heresies* 3.16.1 (*SC* 211, 286, 289f; *ANF* 1:440, 2).

16. Cultured Hellenistic people could disagree on many things regarding the divine, but on one thing they were in agreement: God or the divine was far removed from human contingencies and especially from those feelings and passions which would make one into a powerless prey for the evil designs of others. God is "free from suffering," *apathês.* Cf. page 48 along with references in note 5.

17. One can choose to interpret the text as a *logical* contrasting of the two predicates: for the first *pathetos,* but then next also *apathês.* The remaining section in the account could be understood in such a manner.

18. Robert A. Kraft, *The Apostolic Fathers*, vol. 3, *Barnabas and the Didache* (New York, 1965), 93–94.

19. *Apostolic Constitutions*, 8:12.16: "You said to Your Wisdom: Let Us create . . . ." The same thought is already presupposed in the *Wisdom of Solomon* 9:1f: ". . . . and by Your wisdom have made the human race to have dominion over all Your creation." Compare with the Jewish sources Jacob Jervell, *Imago Dei. Gen 1,26f. im Spätjudentum, in der Gnosis und in den paulinischen Briefen.* Forschungen zur Religion und Literatur des Alten und Neuen Testaments 76 (Göttingen, 1960), 46–50. Another Christian version of the same concept, in which the Jewish undergirding is revealed still more clearly than in Barnabas, is found in Theophilus of Antioch (ca. 180): "God says: 'Let Us create the human race' as though He needed assistance; but He said 'Let Us create' to no one else than His own Logos and Wisdom" (*Ad Autolycum* 2.18; Grant, 56f). Cf. page 70.

20. Barnabas reads *kyrios*, the Lord, instead of *kyros*, 12.10f.

21. Kraft, *Barnabas*, 94.

22. Ibid., 121–22.

23. Justin, *Dialogue* 49.8. Cf. the following rabbinic interpretation: "Rabbi Eleazar said, When will Amalek's name be erased? When idolatry is eradicated along

with all the idolaters and God is acknowledged throughout the whole world as one and His kingdom is established for all eternity" *(Mekhilta de Rabbi Ishmael,* Amalek 2:155–58; Lauterbach, 2:158f).

24. For Christology in the apostolic fathers, see among others Aloys Grillmeier, *Christ in Christian Tradition,* vol. 1, *From the Apostolic Age to Chalcedon (451)* (London, 1965), 36–124; T. E. Pollard, *Johannine Christology and the Early Church* (Cambridge, 1970), 23–48. Especially for angel Christology, see J. Barbel, *Christos Angelos.* Theophaneia. Beiträge zur Religions– und Kirchengeschichte des Altertums 3 (Bonn, 1941), 2d rev. ed. 1964. In an intended large work, Martin Werner sought to maintain the position that angel Christology was the original Christology in the pre-Nicene church *(Die Entstehung des christlichen Dogmas,* 1941). This viewpoint has met with strong and justified criticism. See especially W. Michaelis, *Zur Engelchristologie im Urchristentum, Abbau der Konstruktion Martin Werners* (Basel, 1942). For angel Christology in Hermas, there is an interesting article by H. Moxnes, "God and His Angel in the Shepherd of Hermas," *Studia Theologica* 28 (1974): 49–56.

25. This common designation appeared at the end of the seventeenth century without any comprehensive agreement as to which writings belonged in this category. In addition to those already mentioned, the following are also often included: *The Epistle of Polycarp* (115–130?), possibly two letters—exhortations to the Christian life and a recommendation of the letters of Ignatius; *The Martyrdom of Polycarp,* no doubt first written shortly after the events which took place ca. 156 (later it was enlarged and edited); *The Letter to Diognetus* (170?), a short Christian apology, perhaps directed to Marcus Aurelius' philosophy teacher, Diognetus.

26. *enoptrizometha*—cf. *Wisdom* 7:26. Wisdom is *esoptron* ... *tes tou theou energeias.*

27. Robert M. Grant and Holt H. Graham, *The Apostolic Fathers,* vol. 2, *First and Second Clement* (New York, 1965), 63–64.

28. Note especially the parallel to *Wisdom* 7:26. Wisdom is "an emanation of the eternal light." We also encounter wisdom terminology in a parallel section of *2 Clement* 1:4–8, which concludes with the following statement about Christ: "He called us before we even existed and desired that out of nothing, we should come into existence"—a clear statement of creation! (Loeb 1:130–31).

29. "The Holy Spirit which pre-exists *(to proon),* which created all creation, did God make to dwell in the flesh which He willed." *(Sim.* 5.6.5; Loeb 2:166–67).

30. *Sim.* 8:3.1–2; Loeb 2:194–97.

31. I am here pointing to J. Betz, "Die Eucharistie in der Didache," *Archiv für Liturgiewissenschaft,* 11 (1969), 21–22; K.–G Sandelin, "Vishetens måltid," *Judendom och kristendom under de første århundradena* (Stavanger, 1986), 1:268–83.

32. See my doctoral dissertation, *The Proof from Prophecy: A Study in Justin Martyr's Proof-Text Tradition.* Supplement to Novum Testamentum 56 (Leiden, 1987); and the more popular account in my book *Da Skriften ble åpnet. Den første kristne tolkning av Det gamle testamente* (Oslo, 1987), especially 57–107.

33. *ANF* 1:173.1.

34. J. N. D. Kelly cites this text as one of several examples of "the creeds of St. Justin," *Early Christian Creeds* (3d ed., 1972), 74.

35. Fragment 6 = Clement of Alexandria, *Stromateis* 6.15.128; *ANF* 2:510.1.

36. *ANF* 1:330.2.

37. A striking confirmation of this lies in the fact that all of the eastern baptismal creeds (which are not messianic-oriented in the second article in the same manner) have *Iesous Christos,* where *Christos* obviously is understood as a name.

38. The only place in the *First Apology* where the Scriptural argument for preexistence is advanced by Justin, in a manner similar to the *Dialogue with Trypho,* is a tangential excursus about demonic imitations of Biblical declarations (*1 Apol.* 62–63). It would seem that Justin gathers this material from other sources than what he ordinarily uses in the *First Apology.*

39. The list is borrowed from J. Briérre Narbonne's noteworthy source collection *Exegèse talmudique des prophéties messianiques* (Paris, 1934), 34–35. The great age for this exegetical tradition can be substantiated for most of the texts through the Qumran Dead Sea Scrolls and other early Jewish documents. For details, see my doctoral dissertation, *The Proof from Prophecy,* 262ff; and my article "Schriftbeweis und christologisches Kerygma in der ältesten kirchlichen Schriftauslegung" in Heinrich Kraft, ed., *Schrift und Auslegung.* Veröffentlichungen der Luther-Akademie e.V. Ratzeburg 10 (Erlangen, 1987), 45–54.

40. They appear in the later books of the New Testament. Cf. my article cited in the previous note.

41. I do not find it necessary to go into a detailed analysis here of the very complicated question of the role which Isaiah 53 might have played in Jewish expectations of the Messiah or how this chapter generally was interpreted. See, among others, J. Briérre Narbonne, *Le Messie souffrant dans la litterature rabbinique* (Paris, 1950); H. W. Wolff, *Jesaja 53 im Urchristentum,* 3rd ed. (Berlin, 1952); W. Zimmerli and J. Jeremias, *"pais theou," Theologisches Wörterbuch zum Neuen Testament* (1954), 5:653–713; E. Fascher, *Jesaja 53 in christlicher und jüdischer Sicht* (Berlin, 1958). I contend that the disciples' dismayed rejection of Jesus' warnings about His forthcoming death reveal that the thought of a dying Messiah was foreign to them. No doubt the thought of a messianic redemptive death was also foreign to the dominating hermeneutical tradition among the rabbis. But here the source material is confusing.

42. The list contains a certain element of reconstruction in that the material in the Dialogue which seems to derive from the same Christological tradition followed in the Apology is here included. See *The Proof from Prophecy,* 140–52.

43. A detailed discussion is to be found in my doctoral dissertation; and a more condensed and popular discussion in *Da Skriften ble åpnet,* 66–79.

44. English translation by J. Armitage Robinson, *St. Irenaeus, The Demonstration of the Apostolic Preaching* (London, 1920).

45. See, for example, J. P. Smith, "Hebrew Christian Midrash in Iren. Epid. 43e," *Biblica* 38 (1957), 24–34.

46. Lapide, *Jøder og kristne,* 94. Compare pp. 14–15.

47. See Adolf von Harnack, *Marcion. Das Evangelium von fremden Gott,* 2d ed. (Leipzig, 1924). Texte und Untersuchungen zur Geschichte der altchristlichen Literatur 45 = Darmstadt, 1985, 66–67.

48. See, among others, Hans von Campenhausen, *The Formation of the Christian Bible,* trans. J. A. Baker (Philadelphia, 1972), 80–102; S. Giversen, "Gnostisk skriftforståelse," in Sten Hidal et al., eds., *Judendom och kristendom under de första århundradena* (Stavanger, 1986), 2:77–92.

49. *ANF* 1:249.

50. A. T. Hanson has contended in several of his books and articles that Christ was regarded from the earliest of Christian times as the active subject in Old Testament salvation history. See, among others, *Jesus Christ in the Old Testament* (London, 1965); *The New Testament Interpretation of Scripture* (London, 1980). Hanson's very general statement of this position when viewed from the primary sources is untenable. A clear "theophany Christology" can in any case first be discerned in Justin, which, I would contend, is partially derived from his own theological reflection. See *The Proof from Prophecy,* 409–24.

51. *suum plasma in semetipsum recapitulans.*

52. *Against Heresies* 4.6.2; *SC* 100:440–41; *ANF* 1:468.1. Here and in several similar passages in Justin lies the heart of Irenaeus' later well-known "recapitulation theology."

53. For what follows, see my articles, "The Conversion of Justin Martyr," *Studia Theologica* 30 (1976), 53–73; and "Åpenbaring utenfor åpenbaringen? Antikk religion, gresk filosofi og kristen tro ifølge Justin Martyr," *Tidsskrift for teologi og kirke* 49 (1978), 261–82.

54. *ANF* 1:164.2. Cf. *Jub.* 4.15.22; 5.1–11; 10.1–14; *1 Enoch* 6–16, 86, and esp. 19:1 "Here shall stand in many different appearances the spirits of the angels which have united themselves with women. They have defiled the people and will lead them into error so that they will offer sacrifices to the demons as unto gods. . . ." *Old Testament Pseudepigrapha,* 1:23.

55. *ANF* 1:164.2.

56. *Mekhilta de rabbi Ishmael,* Pisha 5:40–43; Lauterbach 1:36–37; *TB Meg.* 13a (Soncino trans. 74); *Sifre Deut.* #28; *TB Kidd.* 40a (Soncino trans. 199). The latter citation reads: "Idolatry is so abominable that the one who renounces it is reckoned as one who acknowledges the whole Law." Cf. *The Proof from Prophecy,* 366–369.

57. Cf. the early Jewish and rabbinic legends collected in Ginzberg, *Legends* 1:198–201.

58. *ANF* 1:178.1–2.

59. In an interesting study of the figure of Socrates in early Christian literature, E. Benz says that it is impossible to understand *(unerfindlich)* why Justin includes Abraham in his list of those who were persecuted for their break with idolatry. See "Christus und Sokrates in der alten Kirche. Ein Beitrag zum altkirchlichen Verständnis des Märtyrers und des Martyriums," *Zeitschrift für die neutestamentliche Wissenschaft* 43 (1950/51), 195–224. It is certainly not "unerfindlich" if one presupposes the Jewish Abrahamic legends as a background.

60. In addition to the two (not more!) texts in *2 Apology* 8:3 and 13:3 where Justin employs this expression, allow me to cite my somewhat comprehensive discussion of the *Logos spermatikos* concept in my article "Åpenbaring utenfor åpenbaringen?" (cited in note 53) especially 268–273. A bibliography of the copious literature on the subject is also included.

61. *ANF* 1:268.2.

62. *ANF* 1:255.2.
63. *endiatheton en tois splangchnois.*
64. This refers to the previous chapter where Theophilus has related how through Wisdom, the prophets spoke of the world's creation in full agreement with the prophetic picture in *Wisdom* 7:27. On the whole, there are many similarities between Theophilus' concept of wisdom and that which we find in the *Wisdom of Solomon.*
65. Grant, *Theophilus,* 38–41.
66. Ibid., 52–53.
67. Cited above, endnote 19. Theophilus operates in reality with a model that had to result in a *double* agent of creation, through the Son and the Spirit. This viewpoint is found fully developed in Irenaeus. He also tries to distinguish between the role of the Son and the Spirit as agents of creation: "Thus there is shown forth One God, the Father, not made, invisible, creator of all things, above whom there is no other God, and after whom there is no other God. And, since God is rational (*logikos*), by the Word [*Logos*] He created the things that were made; and God is Spirit, and by the Spirit He adorned all things, as also the prophet says: 'By the [*Word*] of the Lord were the heavens established, and by His *Spirit* all their power.' [Ps. 33:6]. Since the Word establishes, that is to say, gives body and grants the reality of being, and the Spirit gives order and form to the diversity of the powers, rightly and fittingly the Word is called the Son, and the Spirit the Wisdom of God. Well also does Paul His apostle say: 'One God, the Father, who is over all and through all and in us all.' For *over all* is the Father; and *through all* is the Son, for through Him all things were made by the Father; and *in us all* is the Spirit, who cries *Abba Father,* and fashions man into the likeness of God. Now the Spirit shows forth the Word, and therefore the prophets announced the Son of God; and the Word utters the Spirit, and therefore is Himself the announcer of the prophets and leads and draws men to the Father." Irenaeus, *Demonstration* 5; J. Armitage Robinson, trans., *St. Irenaeus: The Demonstration of the Apostolic Preaching* (London, 1920), 73–74. A beautiful trinitarian text!
68. Grant, *Theophilus,* 62–65.
69. This is evident from the first chapter.
70. James M. Robinson, ed., *The Nag Hammadi Library* (San Francisco, 1981), 406–16. For the general theme of persecution and Christology, cf. Elaine Pagels, *The Gnostic Gospels* (New York, 1977), chap. 4: "The Passion of Christ and the Persecution of Christians" (in the paperback ed. 1981, 84–122). This chapter is most worthwhile in an otherwise rather peculiar book.
71. Pagels, *The Gnostic Gospels* (1977 ed.), 90–98.
72. Ibid., 90.
73. *ANF* 1:447.2–448.1.
74. Pagels, *The Gnostic Gospels* (1977 ed.), 101.

Chapter 4: Christology in East and West

1. In a quite positive and instructive review *(IXTHYS,* 1986, 94f) of *Inkarnationen,* Helge Haystrup states that the value of geographical "space" as a classification principle in the Christological debate is limited since several of the Early

Church writers clearly do not fit these geographical parameters. I am in total agreement with Haystrup. Nevertheless, I would still want to maintain that a geographical framework has pedagogical merit for a broad outline of the Christological traditions.

2. The unexcelled new standard work on Early Church creeds as well as the more recent scholarship on creedal development is J.N.D. Kelly, *Early Christian Creeds,* first ed. (London, 1950), which was followed by many revisions and reprintings. I have used the 1972 third edition. Instead of referring to it constantly below, I here cite it once and for all.

3. The old classic position on this was F. Kattenbusch, *Das apostolische Symbol I&II,* (Leipzig, 1894–1900); reprinted (Darmstadt, 1962).

4. Hans Lietzmann, *Symbolstudien I–XIV* in *Kleine Schriften,* III, TU 74 (Berlin, 1962 = Darmstadt, 1966), 189–281.

5. After the New Testament, actually only in Justin, *Dial.* 105; *The Martyrdom of Polycarp* 20; *Epistle to Diognetus* 10 (in the last instance in a Johannine citation!).

6. In addition to the earlier documentation presented on behalf of this point of view, see my article "Nikeamøtets kristologiske formel—politikk og teologi," *Patristica Nordica 1, Religio* 5, (1982), 66–84.

7. See the overview in Grillmeier, *Christ in Christian Tradition,* 1:92–94.

8. The reader has already met Ignatius, but for reasons which I shall return to later, I do not believe he was a typical Antiochene.

9. Cf. esp. the instructive presentation in T. E. Pollard, *Johannine Christology and the Early Church* (Cambridge, 1970), 113–16; as well as R. Lorenz, *Arius judaizans? Untersuchungen zur dogmengeschichtlichen Einordnung des Arius.* Forschungen zur Kirchen- und Dogmengeschichte 31 (Göttingen, 1979). The three classical works are F. Loofs, *Paulus von Samosata* (Leipzig, 1924); G. Bardy, *Paul de Samosate* (Louvain, 1929); H. de Riedmatten, *Les actes du procés de Paul de Samosate* (Freiburg, 1952). I follow these authors with a somewhat conservative evaluation, considering the trustworthiness of the fragmentary primary source evidence.

10. See esp. Bardy, *Paul de Samosate,* 428ff.

11. *verbum homo non erat; in homine habitavit.*

12. Pollard, *Johannine Christology,* 114.

13. Ibid., 115.

14. In many ways, Paul of Samosata's Christology resonates with modern theologians who have intellectual difficulties with the Nicene/Chalcedonian preexistence, and two-nature Christology. Modern attempts to formulate a Christology along the basic lines of Paul of Samosata are to be found in G. W. H. Lampe, *God as Spirit* (Oxford, 1977); and A. T. Hanson, *Grace and Truth,* (London, 1975). They are quite different from each other.

15. Grillmeier, *Christ in Christian Tradition,* 1:344–60.

16. Ibid., 1:217–49, 306–43. I am in large measure dependent on Grillmeier's seminal study of Alexandrian Christology.

17. This is one of the points where Bjarne Skard's very worthwhile study becomes oversimplified and inaccurate: "Since the church's confession is the *via media* between the conservative and liberal factions, the Nicene Creed (325) also had

to have a polemical front "against the conservatives." Here the polemics were directed against Apollinarius: *Inkarnasjonen* (Oslo, 1951), 85–89. This is impossible for chronological reasons. Besides, the theologians who supported the Nicene Creed held to a similar Logos-sarx concept as did Apollinarius. It was only later in the century that Nicene theologians became aware of the dangers lurking in a radically pursued Logos-sarx position.

18. Several recent studies of the Arian controversy have shown that the incarnation was a central concept for Arius and that Arianism was motivated by strong soteriological concerns as well. Besides Grillmeier, *Christ in Christian Tradition*, 183–219, see esp. M. F. Wiles, "In Defense of Arius," *Journal of Theological Studies*, NS 13 (1962), 339–47.

19. I do not mean to say by this that Arius' concept of the incarnation was the only reason for his rejection of the Son's *homoousios*. The concept is also inconceivable on the basis of his doctrine of God as F. Ricken and R. D. Williams have shown: F. Ricken, "Nikaia als Krisis des altchristlichen Platonismus," *Theologie und Philosophie* 44 (1969), 321–41; R. D. Williams, "The Logic of Arianism," *Journal of Theological Studies*, NS 34 (1983), 56–81; ——, *Arius: Heresy and Tradition* (London, 1987). The American scholars, R. C. Gregg and D. E. Groh, in some much discussed studies, have postulated that the primary motif in Arius revolves around soteriology: "Salvation for humanity is *to attain God-likeness* and as 'our salvation's leader,' Christ has first attained this as our prototype. He could not then have been equal to God in the beginning." R. C. Gregg, "The Centrality of Soteriology in Early Arianism," *Anglican Theological Review* 59 (1977), 260–75; D. E. Groh, *Early Arianism. A View of Salvation* (London, 1981). Cf. Ø. Norderval, "Arius redivivus? Tendenser innenfor Arius-forskningen," *Norsk teologisk tidsskrift* 86 (1985), 79–90; and R. D. Williams, *Arius*, 19–20.

20. The question is one of the most disputed issues in Origen scholarship and is especially difficult because of the nature of the textual transmission. Cf. H. Görgemanns and H. Karpp, *Origenes Vier Bücher von den Prinzipien*. Texte zur Forschung 24 (Darmstadt, 1976), 133, n. 15, which includes the most pertinent literature.

21. Various explanations have been attempted. Some, for example, have thought that the controversy with Paul of Samosata drove the followers of Origen to a position farthest "away" from Paul and that in addition there arose an internal opposition within the Origenists against Origen's teaching concerning the preexistence of the soul so that his position about Christ's soul also became suspect (Grillmeier, *Christ in Christian Tradition*, 164–66; and esp. Williams, *Arius*, 153, 160–61). R. Lorenz has argued for the thesis that when Christ's soul was eliminated in the Origenistic system, the Logos had to assume the function which Christ's soul had had in Origen, with the consequence that the Logos in Arius' understanding had to be *created.* See R. Lorenz, *Arius judaizans?*, n. 9, 211–24.

22. See especially Grillmeier, *Christ in Christian Tradition,* 1:333–40, for an instructive analysis of Apollinarius' *fysis* concept.

23. *Peri Pascha* 82–85 (Hall, 44–47); a paraphrase of Genesis 1 and Wisdom 10.

24. *fysei theos on kai anthropos.* Ibid., 4–7.

25. Hall, *Melito of Sardis,* 6–7.

26. Ibid., 54–55.

27. For the Christology of Irenaeus, cf. Grillmeier, *Christ in Christian Tradition,* 1:98–104; Pollard, *Johannine Christology,* 42–48. The two classic treatments are A. Houssiau, *La Christologie de Saint Irénée* (Louvain, 1955); A. Benoit, *Saint Irénée. Introduction à l'étude de sa théologie* (Paris, 1960). An interesting account is also found in Gustav Wingren, *Människa och Inkarnationen enligt Irenaeus* (Lund, 1947); ———, *Människan och kristen. En bok em Irenaeus* (Alvsjö, 1983). Regarding Irenaeus' Christology, Grillmeier states: "Irenaeus' Christology . . . shows how firmly he is tied to tradition, especially to the tradition of Asia Minor and of Rome" (100). "It is with Irenaeus above all that he is agreed in emphasizing the unity of Christ. He uses a phrase which will occur some seven times even in the Chalcedonian Definition, 'Christ, one and the same' (*heis kai autos*)" (102). "His Logos concept betrays less of the influence of the Greek philosophers than does that of the Apologists before him and the Alexandrians after him" (103).

28. *naturaliter impassibilem existentem. SC* 211:286.9–10; *ANF* 1:440.2.

29. *SC* 211:322.283–97; *ANF* 1:443.2–444.1.

30. *SC* 211:312–14, 203–23; *ANF* 1:442.2–443.1.

31. Grillmeier, *Christ in Christian Tradition,* 1:103.

32. For Noetus and Sabellius, see J. N. D. Kelly, *Early Christian Doctrines,* 4th ed. (London, 1973), 120–23; A. M. Ritter, "Lehre und Dogma in der Alten Kirche," in *Handbuch der Dogmen– und Theologiegeschichte.* Vol. 1: *Die Lehrentwicklung im Rahmen der Katholizität.* C. Andresen, ed. (Göttingen, 1982), 132–33; W. A. Nienert, "Das vornicaenische *homoousios* als Ausdruck der Rechtgläubigkeit," *Zeitschrift für Kirchengeschichte* 90 (1979), 151–75.

33. For Tertullian's Christology, see my article, "Tertullians kristologi i skriftet mot Praxeas," *Ung teologi* (1969), 11–21. When I wrote this article, I had not yet become aware of the great importance wisdom Christology had for Tertullian.

34. *haec est natiuitas perfecta sermonis dum ex Deo procedit.*

35. *corpus sui generis.*

36. No doubt an allusion to the Scriptures. In agreement with several of the Eastern theologians, Tertullian assumes that these metaphors belong to the Scriptures. Where did they come from? From wisdom literature: light/radiation and sun/rays in Wisd. 7:26, 29; spring/flood: God is the spring of Wisdom, Bar. 3:12; root/tree in Prov. 3:18. Wisdom is identified with the tree of life. In the verses that follow, Wisdom is spoken of as an agent of creation. In Sirach 24, all three metaphors are found in one and the same wisdom chapter: Wisdom is *light* (v.32, NO 38); it is a glorious *threesome* (vv. 12ff, NO 13ff); it is a *river of paradise* (vv. 25ff, NO 30ff).

37. *ANF* 3:600.1–603.2; *CCL* 2:1163.2–1168.34.

38. *ANF* 3:34.2–35.1; *CCL* 1:124.41–125.67.

39. One can also say that Tertullian implicitly teaches that Mary was *theotokos* ("Mother of God"). "That, therefore had to be born which was conceived and was to be brought forth; that is to say, the Spirit, whose 'name should be called Emmanuel which, interpreted, is God with us.' Besides, the flesh is not God, so that it could not have been said concerning it, 'That Holy Thing shall be called the Son of God,' but only that Divine Being who was born in the flesh. . . . Now what Divine Person was born in it? The Word, and the Spirit which became

incarnate with the Word by the will of the Father." (*Against Praxeas* 27.5–6 = *ANF* 3:623.2; *CCL* 2:1198–99, 23–31).

40. *ANF* 3:624.

41. *ANF* 3:626–27.

42. In his review of *Inkarnationen* (see note 1), Helge Haystrup notes that I here make Tertullian into too much of a typical representative of the Western church while "the perhaps not so 'typical' Novatian is completely omitted." I must agree in part with Haystrup. Tertullian was undoubtedly in many ways an independent *Einzelgänger* (free spirit, loner) and to a certain degree ahead of his time, while later Latin theologians like Novatian and Lactantius can be said to be more "primitive" in their Christology. In many ways, they remind one of the apologists. But when Western theology at a later occasion, once for all made its influence felt in an Eastern church controversy, it was *Tertullian's* voice which was heard. It occurred in Pope Leo's Tome to Flavian immediately prior to the Council of Chalcedon (see below).

Chapter 5: The Nicene Confession of Christ

1. *synparchei ho hyios agennêtôs tô theô, aeigennês, agennêtogenês.*

2. Arius' letter to Eusebius of Nicomedia (ca. 318); *NPNF* 3:41.1; *Urkunde* 1:2. 1–3; *New Eusebius* 324–25. I also cite here the quite detailed lisiting of primary sources and secondary literature regarding the Council of Nicea found in my two articles: "Nikeamotets kristologiske formel-politikk og teologi," *Patristica Nordica 1*. Religio 5, Skrifter utgivna av Teologiska Institutionen i Lund (Lund, 1982), 66–84; and "A Neglected Detail in the Creed of Nicea (325)," *Vigiliae Christianae* 41 (1987), 34–54.

3. The best account of the inner logic of Arius' trinitarian concept of which I am aware is R.D. Williams' two studies cited in note 4:19. Two seminal historical studies are G. C. Stead, "The Platonism of Arius," *Journal of Theological Studies,* NS 15 (1964), 16–31; F. Ricken, "Nikaia als Krisis des altchristlichen Platonismus," *Theologie und Philosophie,* 44 (1969), 321–41. While Ricken and Stead view Arius chiefly as a philosophizing theologian who logically carries through the subordinationist strain already found in Origen's Platonic hypostatic thinking, Williams contends that Arius becomes more comprehensible if one assumes that on account of his Aristotelian presuppositions, he could no longer share the Origen-Platonic image concept in determining the relation between the Father and the Son. This latter explanation seems to explain in a more satisfactory manner the quite radical break with the Origen tradition which in fact is the case with Arius when he describes the Logos as a *created being.* There is hardly any sudden passage from Origen to Arius on this point, and one can hardly explain this break satisfactorily by referring to a "radicalization" of Origenistic subordinationism like many scholars have done. Harnack saw this: "It clearly follows from this (i.e., the rejection of wisdom Christology, cf. below), that the doctrine of Origen does not constitute the basis of the system ... and that what it has in common with the orthodox system is not what is really characteristic of it but is on the contrary what is secondary" (*History of Dogma,* 4:40; *Lehrbuch,* 5th ed., 1931, 2:221).

4. I am especially indebted to Williams in this interpretive rendering of the ar-

gumentation that must be reconstructed on account of the scattered Arius-fragments.

5. This verb occasioned considerable difficulty for the Nicene, as well as the pre-Nicene theologians, like Dionysius of Rome. They could not return to the Hebrew text where it clearly read *qanani*, which could just as well, or perhaps even rather, mean "give birth to." Cf. the verbs in Prov. 8:23–30.

6. Harnack was, on the whole, surprisingly negative in his evaluation of Arius: "A son who is no son, a Logos who is no Logos, a monotheism which nevertheless does not exclude polytheism, two or three ousias which are to be revered, while yet only *one* of them is really distinct from the creatures, and indefinable being who first becomes God by becoming man and who is yet neither God nor man, and so on. In every single point we have apparent clearness while all is hollow and formal, a boyish enthusiasm for playing with husks and shells, and a childish self-satisfaction in the working out of empty syllogisms" (*History of Dogma*, 4:41–42; *Lehrbuch* 2:221–22).

7. *Dial.* 128.4 = *ANF* 1:264.1. The same argument and metaphor is found in Tatian, *Oratio* 5 (Whittaker, 10–11).

8. *Pater enim tota substantia est, Filius uero derivatio totius et portio. Against Praxeas* 9.2 = *ANF* 3:603.2–604.1; *CCL* 2:1168.12–13.

9. See Arius' and his friends' letter to Alexander = *Urkunde* 6 in Opitz. "(The Son) is an offspring *(gennema)*, but not as one of the creatures, not as one of those born; nor as Valentinus decreed that the offspring of the Father is an emanation *(probolê)*, nor as the Manicheans taught that the offspring was a portion of the Father, one in essence *(meros homousion tou patros)*; nor as Sabellius, who divides the monad and speaks of a Father-Son; nor as Hieracus, lighted as a torch from another torch, or as a lamp from a lamp so that two would arise (within God)...." *Urkunde* 6:3; 12:10–13:1; *NPNF* 4:458.1–2; also William G. Rusch ed., *The Trinitarian Controversy* (Philadelphia, 1980), 31. It is interesting to note the context Arius gives for the concept *homoousios*, i.e., the old metaphor of the apologists and Tertullian which he here seeks to discredit by associating it with recognized heretics.

10. *Urkunde* 17:32–35; *NPNF* 1:515.2–518.2; *New Eusebius*, 332–34.

11. *Hist. eccl.* 1.7. Cf. V. C. deClerq, *Osius of Cordova. A Contribution to the History of the Constantinian Period.* The Catholic University of America, Studies in Antiquity 13 (Washington, 1954), 203, n. 272.

12. This synod in Antioch, held only a few months before the Council of Nicea, is known through a synodical letter preserved in a Syrian translation which E. Schwarz first published in *Nachrichten von der königlichen Gesellschaft der Wissenschaften zu Göttingen, phil.-hist. Klasse* (Göttingen, 1905), 257–99; later reprinted in *Gesammelte Schriften* (Berlin, 1959), 3:117–68. Nearly all scholars now acknowledge the genuineness of the synodical letter. The text is found in *Urkunde* 18:36–41 and in *New Eusebius* 334–36.

13. *Urkunde* 14:19–29; *NPNF* 3:35.1–41.1; *New Eusebius* 328–30.

14. *Urkunde* 22:42–47; *NPNF* 4:74.1–76.2; *New Eusebius* 344–47.

15. H. Lietzmann, *Symbolstudien*, 60–71.

16. Kelly, *Early Christian Creeds*, 220–30.

17. *De decretis Nicaenae Synodi*, esp. chaps. 19–20 (Greek text in H. G. Opitz, *Athanasius, De Decretis Nicænæ Synodi* (Leipzig, 1935), 15–16; English trans.

NPNF 4:162.2–164.1); and *Ep. ad Afros,* chaps. 5–6 (English trans. *NPNF* 4:491. 1–492.1).

18. I have sought to document this in detail in my article in *Patristica Nordica* 1:70–72.

19. Greek text: *Urkunde* 22:44.11–45.4; Kelly, *Early Christian Creeds,* 215–216.

20. See esp. H. Kraft, "OMOOUSIOS," *Zeitschrift für Kirchengeschichte* 66 (1954/ 55), 1–24; and W. A. Bienert's study cited in chap. 4, n. 32. It is of interest to note here that *the Antiochene tradition* was continuously sympathetic to the homoousios concept. Several sources state that Paul of Samosata spoke of the Logos as homoousios with the Father. It is in and of itself quite trustworthy. Homoousios must no doubt have been a well-suited term for Paul when it came to emphasizing the unity of Wisdom/Logos with God. As a divine attribute, the Logos was a part of the very essence of God. Paul would therefore hardly have had any problem with accepting this declaration in the Nicene Creed. All the great Antiochenes in the fourth and fifth centuries were orthodox Nicenes with regard to the preexistent Logos. But on another point, Paul would have undoubtedly had problems with the Nicene Creed. It was the unambiguous declaration of the creed that the subject of Jesus' suffering, death, and resurrection was the one and the same Logos who was of the same essence as the Father. Here Paul would have had great reservations. The opponents of Antiochene theology felt that the Antiochenes continued to have reservations even after Nicea.

21. One can see both moving and quite unsympathetic examples of this in the last section of Eusebius' letter. *Urkunde* 22 (cf. note 14 above).

22. For Athanasius and Cyril's Christology, cf. esp. Grillmeier, *Christ in Christian Tradition,* 308–28, 473–83; and H. Haystrup, "Kristologien hos Cyril af Alexandria," *Patristica Nordica 1.* Religio 5, Skrifter utgivna av Teologiska Institutionen i Lund (Lund, 1982), 7–20.

23. *quod non est assumptus, non est sanatus.* For the Cappadocian polemic against Apollinarius, see esp. H. Haystrup, *Kristusbekendelsen i Oldkirken,* 2 ed. (Copenhagen, 1982), 65–89; Grillmeier, *Christ in Christian Tradition* 1:367–77.

24. See my article: "Gudsbildet i oldkirkens teologi," *Tidskrift for teologi og kirke* 48 (1977), 179–92.

25. *unum ex trinitate secundum carem crucifixum.* Cf. Grillmeier, *Christ in Christian Tradition,* 1:521.

Chapter 6: The Chalcedonian Definition of Christ (451)

1. John Chrysostom was, for example, an avowed Alexandrian in Christology.

2. *Five Catechetical Sermons* (426). Here, and in the following, I render the passages from Theodore as cited in Grillmeier, *Christ in Christian Tradition,* 344ff.

3. Ibid., 346.

4. Ibid.

5. Ibid.

6. Ibid.

7. Ibid., 349.

8. Ibid., 350.

9. Ibid., 354–55.

10. Ibid., 373.

11. Ibid., 346. See also Jaroslav Pelikan, *The Emergence of the Catholic Tradition (100–600)* (Chicago, 1971), 264–68; and Justo L. Gonzalez, *A History of Christian Thought,* 1:368–78.

12. An account of Ephesus II (449 A.D.) is to be found in W. H. C. Frend, *The Rise of Christianity* (Philadelphia, 1984), 766–70.

13. Henry Bettenson, *Documents of the Christian Church,* 2d ed. (New York, 1947), 68–69.

14. Grillmeier, *Christ in Christian Tradition,* 1:481.

15. Two distinguished accounts of Leo's Tome are ibid., 460–77; and Haystrup, *Kristusbekendelsen,* 133ff.

16. *agit utraque forma cum alterius communione quod proprium est.*

17. "... die Kirche des orients war um ihren Glauben gebracht." Harnack's analysis of the Council of Chalcedon and its creed is to be found in *History of Dogma,* 4:212–26. The citation is from 222.

18. See esp. A. M. Ritter's account in *Handbuch der Dogmengeschichte,* C. Andresen, ed. (Göttingen, 1982), 1:261ff.

19. Grillmeier, *Christ in Christian Tradition,* 1:481.

20. Cf., e.g., Haystrup, *Kristusbekendelsen,* 150–56.

21. Cf. Grillmeier, " 'Piscatorie'—'Aristotelice.' Zur Bedeutung der 'Formel' in den seit Chalkedon getrennten Kirchen," *Mit ihm und in ihm. Christologische Forschungen und Perspektiven* (Freiburg, 1975), 283–300. Grillmeier states that when all the replies had come in, about 470 had subscribed, though not all the answers are extant.

22. Grillmeier, "Piscatorie," *Mit ihm und in ihm,* 285.

23. This is strongly and correctly asserted by Elert in his indepth analysis of the latter phase of the Christological debate. More and more, it was *the synoptic* Jesus and especially the temptation narrative and the struggle in Gethsemane which came to stand in the center of the debate as to how the Nicene-Cyrillian Christology was to be understood. Werner Elert, *Der Ausgang der altkirchlichen Christologie* (Berlin, 1957), esp. 151–69, 230–59.

24. There is a detailed and lively account of this in Frend, *The Rise of Christianity,* 837–56; and Haystrup, *Kristusbekendelsen,* 157–85.

25. Cf. esp. F. Heinzer, *Gottes Sohn als Mensch. Die Struktur des Menschseins Christi bei Maximus Confessor.* Paradosis. Beiträge zur Geschichte der altchristlichen Literatur und Theologie 26. (Freiburg, 1980); also Elert, *Ausgang.*

26. The best of the newer introductions to the Athanasian Creed is to be found in J. N. D. Kelly, *The Athanasian Creed* (London, 1964). The Latin text is to be found in Philip Schaff, ed., *The Creeds of Christendom* (New York, 1889; repr. Grand Rapids, n.d.), 2:66–70.

Postscript: The Existential Significance of the Incarnation

1. Respectively, from Bultmann's well-known manifesto of 1941, *New Testament and Mythology,* trans. Schubert M. Ogden (Philadelphia, 1984), 1–3; and from an article ten years later entitled, "The Message of Jesus and the Problem of

Mythology," in *Jesus Christ and Mythology* (New York, 1958), 16–17.

2. John Hick, ed., *The Myth of God Incarnate* (London, 1977).

3. I do not believe it necessary to give a detailed bibliography of the debate. A few titles should suffice to highlight the issues: M. Green, ed., *The Truth of God Incarnate* (London, 1977), published only six weeks after "The Myth"!; G. W. H. Lampe, *God as Spirit* (Oxford, 1977); M. Goulder, ed., *Incarnation and Myth: The Debate Continued* (Grand Rapids, 1979); A. Nichols, *The Art of God Incarnate* (London, 1980); J. D. G. Dunn, *Christology in the Making* (Philadelphia, 1980); A. T. Hanson, *The Image of the Invisible God* (London, 1982); R. H. Fuller and P. Perkins, *Who Is This Christ? Gospel Christology and Contemporary Faith* (Philadelphia, 1983); B. Hebblethwaite, *The Incarnation. Collected Essays in Christology* (Cambridge, 1987).

4. Cf., e.g., C. Colpe, *Die religionsgeschichtliche Schule. Darstellung und Kritik ihres Bildes vom gnostischen Erlösermythus*. Forschungen zur Religion und Literatur des Alten und Neuen Testaments NF 60 (Göttingen, 1961); and Sverre Aalen's review of this book in *Tidsskrift for teologi og kirke* 36 (1965), 241–43; E. M. Yamauchi, *Pre-Christian Gnosticism. A Survey of the Proposed Evidences* (London, 1973).

5. See the very enlightening presentation in W. Jaeger, *The Theology of the Early Greek Philosophers* (Oxford, 1947).

6. This, I contend, must be said with emphasis against Vermes' *Jesus the Jew*, which otherwise is interesting precisely because he honestly seeks to place Jesus into the Jewish context of first century Palestine.

Glossary

Allegory: a figurative story or text. An interpretation which presupposes that the text being interpreted is intended to be figurative is called *allegorical.*

Catechumen: baptismal candidate who is being instructed in the Christian faith.

Christology: doctrine about Christ, confession of Christ.

Creation, Agent of: When it is said of Christ that everything has been created "through Him," that is, through His mediation, we call Christ the agent of creation.

Creed: a short confession of faith.

Emanation: a substance which radiates out from another.

Eschatology, eschatological: that which has to do with the endtimes, the last things (Greek: *ta eskata*).

Homoousios: "of the same essence as" or "consubstantial with."

Hypostasis: see page 81.

Incarnation: "the taking on of flesh"—that God's Son became a human being and came "in the flesh," *in carne.*

Messianism: the Jewish notion about and expectation of a Messiah.

Modalism: see page 90.

Preexistence: The Son's presence with the Father before He became a human being.

Prosopon: see page 81.

Sabellianism: see page 90.

Typology, typological: an interpretation of Biblical passages that views previous happenings in the history of the people of God as archetypes or prototypes for later events.

Bibliography

Aalen, Sverre. *Guds Sønn og Guds rike. Nytestamentlige studier.* Oslo, 1973.

Barbel, J. *Christos Angelos.* Theophaneia Beiträge zur Religions- und Kirchengeschichte des Altertums 3. Bonn, 1941. 2d rev. ed., 1964.

Bardy, G. *Paul de Samosate.* Louvain, 1929.

Bauer, Walter. *Das Leben Jesu im Zeitalter der neutestamentlichen Apokryphen.* Tübingen, 1909.

Benoit, A. *Saint Irénée. Introduction à l'étude de sa théologie.* Paris, 1960.

Benz, E. "Christus und Sokrates in der alten Kirche. Ein Beitrag zum altkirchlichen Verständnis des Märtyrers und des Martyriums." *Zeitschrift für die neutestamentliche Wissenschaft* 43 (1950/51): 195–224.

Berger, D. and M. Wyshogrod. *Jews and "Jewish Christianity."* New York, 1978.

Berger, K. "Die königlichen Messiastraditionen des Neuen Testaments." *New Testament Studies* 20 (1974): 1–44.

Bettenson, Henry. *Documents of the Christian Church.* New York, 1947.

Betz, J. "Die Eucharistie in der Didache." *Archiv für Liturgiewissenschaft* 11 (1969).

Betz, O. *What Do We Know About Jesus?* London, 1968.

Bickermann, Elias. *Der Gott der Makkabäer.* Berlin, 1937. English translation, *From Ezra to the Last of the Maccabees.* New York, 1962.

Bienert, W. A. "Das vornicaenische *homoousios* als Ausdruck der Rechtgläubigkeit." *Zeitschrift für Kirchengeschichte* 90 (1979): 151–75.

Bousset, Wilhelm. *Kyrios Christos. Geschichte des Christusglaubens von den Anfängen bis Irenäus.* Göttingen, 1913. English translation by John E. Steely, *A History of the Belief in Christ from the Beginning of Christianity to Irenaeus.* Nashville, 1970.

Brown, R. E. *The Gospel According to John (i–xii).* New York, 1966.

Bultmann, Rudolf. *Jesus Christ and Mythology.* New York, 1958.

———. *New Testament and Mythology.* Translated by Schubert M. Ogden. Philadelphia, 1984.

Burney, C. F. "Christ as the APXH of Creation (Prov VII 22, Col I 15–18, Rev III 14)." *Journal of Theological Studies* 27 (1926): 160–77.

BIBLIOGRAPHY

Cabaniss, A. "Wisdom 18, 14f.: An Early Christmas Text." *Vigiliae Christianae* 10 (1956): 97–102.

Campenhausen, Hans von. *Die Entstehung der christlichen Bibel.* Beiträge zur historischen Theologie 39. Tübingen, 1968. English translation by J. A. Baker, *The Formation of the Christian Bible.* Philadelphia, 1972.

Chadwick, Henry, ed. *Origen: Contra Celsum.* Cambridge, 1965.

Charlesworth, James H., ed. *The Old Testament Pseudepigrapha.* 2 vols. New York, 1983–85.

Christ, F. *Jesus Sophia. Die Sophia-Christologie bei den Synoptikern.* Arbeiten zur Theologie des Alten und Neuen Testaments 57. Zürich, 1970.

Colpe, C. *Die religionsgeschichtliche Schule. Darstellung und Kritik ihres Bildes vom gnostischen Erlösermythus.* Forschungen zur Religion und Literatur des Alten und Neuen Testaments NF 60. Göttingen, 1961.

Danby, H. *The Mishnah.* Oxford, 1933.

de Clerq, V. C. *Ossius of Cordova. A Contribution to the History of the Constantinian Period.* The Catholic University of America, Studies in Antiquity 13. Washington, 1954.

Duling, D. C. "Solomon, Exorcism, and the Son of David." *Harvard Theological Review* 68 (1975): 235–52.

———. "The Promises to David and their Entrance into Christianity: Nailing Down a Likely Hypothesis." *New Testament Studies* 20 (1973/74): 55–77.

Dunn, James D. G. *Christology in the Making. A New Testament Inquiry Into the Origins of the Doctrine of the Incarnation.* Philadelphia, 1980.

Ehrenpreis, Marcus. *Talmud, Fariseism, Urkristendom.* n.p., 1933.

Elert, W. *Der Ausgang der altkirchliche Christologie.* Berlin, 1957.

Epstein, I. *Judaism. A Historical Presentation.* Baltimore, 1968.

———, ed. *The Babylonian Talmud.* London, 1938–52.

Fascher, E. *Jesja 53 in christlicher und jüdischer Sicht.* Berlin, 1958.

Freedman, H., ed. *Midrash Rabba I-X.* London, 1939ff.

Frend, W. H. C. *The Rise of Christianity.* Philadelphia, 1984.

Fuller, R. H. and P. Perkins. *Who Is This Christ? Gospel Christology and Contemporary Faith.* Philadelphia, 1983.

Ginzberg, L. *The Legends of the Jews.* Vols. 4, 6. Philadelphia, 1968.

Giversen, S. "Gnostisk skriftforståelse," in *Judendom och kristendom under de första århundradena,* Sten Hidal, ed., et al. Vol. 2. Stavanger, 1986.

Goldberg, A. M. *Untersuchungen über die Vorstellung von der Schekhinah in der frühen rabbinischen Literatur—Talmud und Midrasch.* Studia

Judaica. Forschungen zur Wissenschaft des Judentums 5. Berlin, 1969.

Gonzalez, Justo L. *A History of Christian Thought.* Vol. 1. Nashville, 1970.

Goodspeed, E. J. *Die ältesten Apologeten. Texte mit kurzen Einleitungen.* Göttingen, 1914. Reprint ed. 1984.

Görgemanns, H. and H. Karpp. *Origenes Vier Bücher von den Prinzipien.* Texts zur Forschung 24. Darmstadt, 1976.

Goulder, M., ed. *Incarnation and Myth: The Debate Continued.* Grand Rapids, 1979.

Grant, Robert M. *The Early Doctrine of God.* Charlottesville, 1966.

——, ed. *Theophilus of Antioch Ad Autolycum.* Oxford, 1970.

Green, M., ed. *The Truth of the God Incarnate.* London, 1977.

Gregg, R. C. "The Centrality of Soteriology in Early Arianism." *Anglican Theological Review* 59 (1977): 260–75.

Grillmeier, Aloys. *Christ in Christian Tradition.* Vol. 1, *From the Apostolic Age to Chalcedon (451).* London, 1965.

——. " 'Piscatorie'—'Aristotelice.' Zur Bedeutung der 'Formel' in den seit Chalkedon getrennten Kirchen," chap. in *Mit ihm und in ihm. Christologische Forschungen und Perspektiven.* Freiburg, 1975.

Groh, D. E. *Early Arianism. A View of Salvation.* London, 1981.

Hall, S. G., ed. *Melito of Sardis: On Pascha and Fragments.* Oxford Early Christian Texts. Oxford, 1979.

Hamerton-Kelly, R. G. *Pre-Existence, Wisdom, and The Son of Man. A Study of the Idea of Pre-Existence in the New Testament.* Society for New Testament Studies, Monograph Ser. 21. Cambridge, 1973.

Hanson, A. T. *Grace and Truth.* London, 1975.

——. *Jesus Christ in the Old Testament.* London, 1965.

——. *The New Testament Interpretaion of Scripture.* London, 1980.

——. *The Image of the Invisible God.* London, 1982.

Harnack, Adolf von. *Das Wesen des Christentums.* Leipzig, 1900. English translation by Thomas B. Saunders, *What Is Christianity?* New York, 1957.

——. *Lehrbuch der Dogmengeschichte.* 5th ed. Tübingen, 1931. English translation of third German edition by Neil Buchanan, *History of Dogma.* 7 vols. New York, 1961.

——. *Marcion. Das Evangelium von fremden Gott.* 2d ed. Leipzig, 1924.

Haystrup, H. "Kristologien hos Cyril af Alexandria," in *Patristica Nordica 1.* Religio 5. Skrifter utgivna av Teologiska Institutionen i Lund. Lund, 1982. 7–20.

——. *Kristusbekendelsen i Oldkirken.* 2d ed. Copenhagen, 1982.

Hayward, R. *Divine Name and Presence: The Memra*. Totowa, New Jersey, 1981.

Hebblethwaite, B. *The Incarnation. Collected Essays in Christology*. Cambridge, 1987.

Heinzer, F. *Gottes Sohn als Mensch. Die Struktur des Menschseins Christi bei Maximus Confessor*. Paradosis. Beiträge zur Geschichte der altchristlichen Literatur und Theologie 26. Freiburg, 1980.

Hengel, Martin. *Der Sohn Gottes. Die Entstehung der Christologie und die jüdisch-hellenistische Religionsgeschichte*. 2d ed. Tübingen, 1977. English translation by John Bowden, *The Son of God. The Origin of Christology and the History of Jewish-Hellenistic Religion*. Philadelphia, 1976.

————. *Judentum und Hellenismus*. Wissenschaftliche Untersuchungen zum Neuen Testament 10. Tübingen, 1969. English translation by John Bowden, *Judaism and Hellenism*. 2 vols. Philadelphia, 1974.

Hick, John, ed. *The Myth of the God Incarnate*. London, 1977.

Hidal, S., et al. *Judendom och kristendom under de första århundradena*. Stavanger, 1986.

Houssiau, A. *La Christologie de Saint Irénée*. Louvain, 1955.

Jaeger, W. *The Theology of the Early Greek Philosophers*. Oxford, 1947.

Jeremias, J. *Neutestamentliche Theologie. Erster Theil: Die Verkündiging Jesu*. Gütersloh, 1971.

Jervell, Jakob. *Imago Dei. Gen 1,26f. im Spätjudentum, in der Gnosis und in den paulinischen Briefen*. Forschungen zur Religion und Literatur des Alten und Neuen Testaments 76. Göttingen, 1960.

Kattenbusch, F. *Das apostolische Symbol I&II*. Leipzig, 1894/1900.

Kelly, J. N. D. *Early Christian Creeds*. 3d ed. London, 1972.

————. *Early Christian Doctrines*. 4th ed. London, 1973.

————. *The Athanasian Creed*. London, 1964.

Kraft, H. "HOMOOUSIOS." *Zeitschrift für Kirchengeschichte* 66 (1954/55): 1–24.

Kretschmar, G. *Studien zur frühchristlichen Trinitätstheologie*. Beiträge zur historischen Theologie 21. Tübingen, 1956.

Küchler, M. *Frühjüdische Weisheitraditionen. Zum Fortgang weisheitlichen Denkens im Bereich des frühjüdischen Jahweglaubens*. Orbis biblicus et orientalis 26. Freiburg, 1979.

Kuhn, P. *Gottes Selbsterniedrigung in der Theologie der Rabbinen*. Studien zum Alten und Neuen Testament 17. Munich, 1968.

Lampe, G. W. H. *God as Spirit*. Oxford, 1977.

Lapide, Pinchas. *Jøder og kristne. Bidrag til en dialog*. Oslo, 1978.

Larsson, E. "Kristus och skapelsen i nytestamentligt hymnmaterial." *Deus Creator. Bidrag til skapelsesteologien.* Festskrift for Ivar P. Seierstad, 69–84. Oslo, 1971.

Lasker, Daniel J. *Jewish Philosophical Polemics Against Christianity in the Middle Ages.* New York, 1977.

Lauterbach, J. Z. *Mekilta de-Rabbi Ishmael I–III.* Philadelphia, 1976.

Leivestad, R. "Der apokalyptische Menschensohn ein theologisches Phantom." *Annual of the Swedish Theological Institute* 6 (1968): 49–105.

———. "Er den apokalyptiske menneskesønn en moderne teologiske oppfinnelse?" *Norsk teologisk tidsskrift* 70 (1969): 221–35.

———. *Hvem ville Jesus være.* Oslo, 1982.

Lietzmann, H. *Symbolstudien I–XIV* in *Kleine Schriften* 3. Berlin, 1962.

Lindeskog, Gösta. "Messianologie und Christologie." *Das jüdisch-christliche Problem. Randglossen zu einer Forschungsepoche.* Acta Universitatis Upsaliensis, Historia Religionum 9. Uppsala, 1986. 111–44.

Loofs, F. *Paulus von Samosata.* Leipzig, 1924.

Lorenz, R. *Arius judaizans? Untersuchungen zur dogmengeschichtlichen Einordnung des Arius.* Forschungen zur Kirchen- und Dogmengeschichte 31. Göttingen, 1979.

Lövestam, E. "Jesus Fils de David chez les Synoptiques." *Studia theologica* 28 (1974): 97–109.

Mack, B. L. *Logos und Sophia. Untersuchungen zur Weisheitstheologie im hellenistischen Judentum.* Studien zur Umwelt des Neuen Testaments 10. Göttingen, 1973.

Michaelis, W. *Zur Engelchristologie im Urchristentum. Abbau der Konstruktion Martin Werners.* Basel, 1942.

Moule, C. F. D. *The Origin of Christology.* Cambridge, 1977.

Moxnes, H. "God and His Angel in the Shepherd of Hermas." *Studia Theologica* 28 (1974): 49–56.

Müller, M. *Der Ausdruck 'Menschensohn' in den Evangelien. Voraussetzungen und Bedeutung.* Acta Theologica Danica XVII. Leiden, 1984.

Narbonne, J. Briérre. *Exegèse talmudique des prophéties messianiques.* Paris, 1934.

———. *Le Messie souffrant dans la litterature rabbinque.* Paris, 1950.

Nemoy, Leon. "Al-Qirqisani's Account of the Jewish Sects and Christianity." *HUCA* 7 (1930): 317–97.

Neusner, Jacob. *Midrash in Context. Exegesis in Formative Judaism.* Philadelphia, 1983.

———. *The Rabbinic Traditions about the Pharisees before 70.* 3 vols. Leiden, 1971.

Nichols, A. *The Art of God Incarnate.* London, 1980.

Norderval, Ø. "Arius redivivus? Tendenser innenfor Ariusforskningen." *Norsk teologisk tidsskrift* 86 (1985): 79–90.

Opitz, H. G. *Urkunde zur Geschichte des arianischen Streites 318–28.* Berlin, 1934.

Outler, Albert C., ed. *Augustine: Confessions and Enchiridion.* Library of Christian Classics 7. Philadelphia, n.d.

Pagels, Elaine. *The Gnostic Gospels.* New York, 1977.

Pannenberg, W. "Die Aufnahme des philosophischen Gottesbegriffs als dogmatisches Problem der frühchristlichen Theologie." *Zeitrschrift für Kirchengeschichte* 70 (1959): 1–45.

———. *Grundfragen systematischer Theologie, Gesammelte Aufsätze.* 2d ed. Göttingen, 1971.

Pauly, August F., ed. *Realenzyklopœdie der classischen Altertumswissenschaft.* Supp. 8. Stuttgart, 1956. S.v. "Solomon," by K. Preisendanz.

Pedersen, E. Thestrup. *Jesu forkyndelse.* 4th ed. Copenhagen, 1980.

Pelikan, Jaroslav. *The Emergence of the Catholic Tradition (100–600).* Chicago, 1971.

Pollard, T. E. *Johannine Christology and the Early Church.* Cambridge, 1970.

Prestige, G. L. *God in Patristic Thought.* 2d ed. London, 1952.

Ricken, F. "Nikaia als Krisis des altchristlichen Platonismus." *Theologie und Philosophie* 44 (1969): 321–41.

Riedmatten, H. de. *Les actes du procés de Paul de Samosate.* Freiburg, 1952.

Ringgren, H. *Word and Wisdom. Studies in the Hypostatization of Divine Qualities and Functions in the Ancient Near East.* Lund, 1947.

Ritter, A. M. "Lehre und Dogma in der Alten Kirche," in *Handbuch der Dogmen- und Theologiegeschichte,* C. Andresen, ed., vol. 1, *Die Lehrentwicklung im Rahmen der Katholizität.* Göttingen, 1982.

Roberts, A. and J. Donaldson, eds. *The Ante-Nicene Fathers.* Vols. 1 & 3. Grand Rapids, 1950–51.

Robinson, J. Armitage, ed. *St. Irenaeus, The Demonstration of the Apostolic Preaching.* London, 1920.

Robinson, J. M., ed. *The Nag Hammadi Library.* San Francisco, 1981.

Rusch, William G. *The Trinitarian Controversy.* Philadelphia, 1980.

Sæbø, Magne. "Messianisme hos Kronisten?" in *Israel-Kristus-Kirken.* Festskrift til Sverre Aalen, 53–75. Oslo, 1979.

Sandelin, K. G. "Vishetens måltid." *Judendom och kristendom under de första århundradena.* Vol. 1, 268–83. Stavanger, 1986.

Schaff, Philip. *A Select Library of Nicene and Post-Nicene Fathers.* 2d series, vol. 1. Grand Rapids, 1952.

——. *The Creeds of Christendom.* Vol. 2. New York, 1889.

Schencke, W. *Die Chokma (Sophia) in der jüdischen Hypostasenspekulation.* Skrifter utg. av Det Norske Videnskapsakademi II, 1912 no. 6. Christiania, 1913.

Schimanowski, G. *Weisheit und Messias.* Wissenschaftliche Untersuchungen zum Neuen Testament. 2 Row 17. Tübingen, 1985.

Schubert, K. "Einige Beobachtungen zum Verständnis des Logosbegriffes im frührabbinischen Schrifttum." *Judaica* 9 (1953): 65–80.

Schwarz, E. *Gesammelte Schriften.* Vol. 3. Berlin, 1959.

Skard, Bjarne. *Inkarnasjonen.* Oslo, 1951.

Skarsaune, Oskar. "A Neglected Detail in the Creed of Nicaea (325)." *Vigiliae Christianae* 41 (1987): 34–54.

——. "Åpenbaring untenfor åpenbaringen? Antikk religion, gresk filosofi og kristen tro ifølge Justin Martyr." *Tidsskrift for teologi og kirke* 49 (1978): 261–82.

——. *Da skriften ble åpnet. Den første kristne tolkning av Det gamle testamente.* Oslo, 1987.

——. "Gudsbildet i oldkirkens teologi." *Tidsskrift for teologi og kirke* 48 (1977): 179–92.

——. "Nikeamøtets kristologiske formel—politikk og teologi." *Patristica Nordica 1.* Religio, Skrifter utgivna av Teologiska Institutionen i Lund 5. Lund, 1982. 66–84.

——. "Oldkirkens kristologi og de jødiske frelsesforventningene," in *Judendom och kristendom under de første århundradena.* Vol. 2, 201–19. Stavanger, 1986.

——. "Schriftbeweis und Christologisches Kerygma in der ältesten kirchlichen Schriftauslegung." In *Schrift und Auslegung,* Heinrich Kraft, ed. Veröffentlichungen der Luther-Akademie e.V. Ratzeburg 10. Erlangen, 1987.

——. "The Conversion of Justin Martyr." *Studia Theologica* 30 (1976): 53–73.

——. "Tertullians kristologi i skriftet mot Praxeas." *Ung teologi* (1969): 11–21.

——. *The Proof from Prophecy: A Study in Justin Martyr's Proof Text Tradition.* Supplements to Novum Testamentum 56. Leiden, 1987.

Smith, D. W. *Wisdom Christology in the Synoptic Gospels.* Rome, 1970.

Smith, J. P. "Hebrew Christian Midrash in Iren. Epid. 43é." *Biblica* 38 (1957): 24–34.

Stead, G. C. "The Platonism of Arius." *Journal of Theological Studies* NS 15 (1964): 16–31.

Stevenson, J. *A New Eusebius. Documents Illustrating the History of the Church to A.D. 337.* Rev. ed. London, 1987.

Strack, Hermann L. and Paul Billerbeck. *Kommentar zum Neuen Testament aus Talmud und Midrasch.* 6 vols. Munich, 1922–61.

Suggs, J. M. *Wisdom, Christology and Law in Matthew's Gospel.* Cambridge, 1970.

Talmon, S. "Typen der Messiaserwartung um die Zeitwende." In *Probleme biblischer Theologie. Gerhard von Rad zum 70. Geburtstag,* H. W. Wolff, ed., 571–88. Munich, 1971.

Urbach, E. E. *The Sages—Their Concepts and Beliefs.* Jerusalem, 1975.

Vermes, Geza. *Jesus the Jew. A Historian's Reading of the Gospels.* London, 1973.

Volz, P. *Die Eschatologie der jüdischen Gemeinde im neutestamentlichen Zeitalter.* Tübingen, 1934.

Werner, Martin. *Die Entstehung des christlichen Dogmas.* n.c., 1941.

Whittaker, M., ed. *Tatian: Oratio ad Graecos and Fragments.* Oxford Early Christian Texts. Oxford, 1982.

Wiles, M. F. "In Defence of Arius." *Journal of Theological Studies* NS 13 (1962): 339–47.

Williams, R. D. *Arius: Heresy and Tradition.* London, 1987.

———. "The Logic of Arianism." *Journal of Theological Studies* NS 34 (1983): 56–81.

Windisch, H. "Die göttliche Weisheit der Juden und die Paulinische Christologie." In *Neutestamentliche Studien Georg Heinrici,* A. Deissmann and H. Windisch, eds., 220–34. Leipzig, 1914.

Wingren, Gustav. *Människa och kristen. En bok om Irenaeus.* Alvsjö, 1983.

———. *Människan och Inkarnationen enligt Irenaeus.* Lund, 1947.

Wolff, H. W. *Jesja 53 im Urchristentum.* 3d ed., Berlin, 1952.

Yamauchi, E. M. *Pre-Christian Gnosticism. A Survey of the Proposed Evidences.* London, 1973.

Zimmerli, W. and J. Jeremias. *pais theou, Theologisches Wörterbuch zum NT.* Vol. 5 (Berlin, 1958): 653–713.

Index

Boxed entries in the text are italicized. Only those modern scholars who are mentioned in the text are to be found in the index. The index does not include the notes.

Reflection Questions

The following are more than questions of fact. They call for reflection and careful thought in the light of Skarsaune's book. Not only must the text be read, but rereading or outlining may be a necessary first step for discussing the questions below. The incarnation has broad implications and applications. One purpose for the questions is to show how an essential doctrine can and perhaps should be tied to issues which at first glance do not seem to be related. The questions should not be read as though the answer is implied. A basic presupposition is that the Holy Spirit leads a person to faith through the proclamation of the Gospel. Yet at times one is compelled to use God-given reason and logic, remembering that matters of faith are not contrary *to reason though often* beyond *human comprehension.*

Introduction and Chapter 1

Skarsaune directs chapter 1 against a particular rejection of the incarnation (namely, that it grew out of prevailing Greek and/or Jewish myths of the time), but his introduction places the discussion within the larger context of varied attempts to explain away the unique truth of the incarnation.

What challenges to the incarnation have you experienced from, e.g., humanism? the sciences? various attempts to "modernize" Christianity? New Age proponents? within Protestant denominations?

On pages 14–15, Skarsaune quotes the Jewish scholar Lapide, who says that St. Paul presented *two* explanations of the incarnation: one acceptable to Greeks and another to the Jews. Although the accusation is not the basis for chapter 1, how adequately does the rest of the chapter respond to that contemporary charge?

According to Skarsaune, one explanation of the incarnation

would have been acceptable to the Greeks, and another would have been acceptable to the Jews. Both explanations would have been heretical. What evidence(s) do you see of either explanation being propounded today?

Traditional Christians have been accused of "the suspension of disbelief" in order to deal with those areas of life that are still unpredictable and/or overwhelming. Given Skarsaune's presentation so far, how do you think he might respond to such a challenge?

The concept of the incarnation has been rejected by many because God's activity in the world cannot be verified, much less identified—and, therefore, it may seem more rational to talk of "God" as a "divine spark" within every person. What insights does this chapter provide in response to that charge?

What insights does this chapter provide for the discussion of "a theology of glory" versus "a theology of the cross"?

Chapter 2

Given the point of chapter 1 (that the incarnation could not have arisen out of either Greek or Jewish myths), Skarsaune shows in chapter 2 that the belief did have precedence for acceptance within Judaism, that Jewish intertestamental religious thought could accept a personification/incarnation of God's Wisdom. This precedence for acceptance, however, cannot adequately explain the disciples' belief in and confession of the incarnation; that came because of Jesus' own words and actions about Himself.

While Skarsaune shows that the incarnation was not totally foreign to Jewish thinking at the time of the disciples, what would have to be added to show that the incarnation is the fulfillment of Old Testament prophecy?

In this chapter's section on "The Concept of Wisdom in Judaism," Skarsaune points out that the intertestamental Wisdom literature was developed as a well-thought-out defense against Hellenistic philosophies, which said that the highest ideals for mankind are available to all through human reason, "a universal ethic applicable to all people"—a belief that continues in today's secular humanism.

To what extent is this Greek philosophy true? What are its pluses (as well as it shortcomings) as a practical ground for daily life? for world politics and finance?

Intertestamental Judaism rejected both Platonic and Stoic thought because neither approach to the ideal/wise life was based on the totality of God's will (i.e., the "Law"). In what ways does God's will (which includes that all should come to faith in Christ and be saved) influence your day-to-day interactions/decisions? your hopes for world politics and finance?

Evaluate the validity of saying that the exclusiveness of Christianity as the only way is the logical extension of the exclusiveness claimed by intertestamental Wisdom literature.

Some would challenge Skarsaune for dismissing the charge that the personage of Wisdom is a mere "poetic personification" or literary device. Yet Skarsaune quickly passes over the issue by saying that, literary device or not, the point is that there was precedence for accepting the underlying concept and that the disciples saw the personification actually taking place in Jesus.

If one would assume Skarsaune's line of argument (that the question of Wisdom as a literary device is not as important as that the disciples believed the personification was taking place in Jesus), how would you answer those who today charge that Jesus' own divinity is nothing more than a Biblical literary device? How do our presuppositions about God and our conception of Him affect our answer?

Skarsaune points out that nothing in Jewish philosophy would lead automatically to the necessity of the incarnation. Rather, Jesus' resurrection-enthronement was the primary basis for the disciples' faith and subsequent outreach—a point clearly made, e.g., in 1 Cor. 15:17.

Some have held that the essence of Christianity does not require that the resurrection include a physical resuscitation of Jesus' body. In discussing that point, how might Skarsaune's line of thought be used?

Chapter 3

Skarsaune states that the Jews opposed the concept of a messiah as God incarnate because it is based on a weak God, not on God as the omnipotent creator who bestows the everlasting kingdom on the Messiah.

> Christians too often forget who God is. In what way(s) might the concept of a weak God be reflected in contemporary Christian assumptions/beliefs about "the power of prayer"? about millennialism? about the state of Israel? What response might be effective against contemporary accusations of a weak God?

The Jews opposed the incarnate Messiah concept because it also implied "overstepping of the boundary between God and humanity." Barnabas responded that it was necessary for God (i.e., the agent of creation) to allow Himself to be killed by His own creation, "that this was indeed a divine work that a mere human messiah would have been unable to accomplish."

> Luther saw this "high" view of God's transcendence in the Zwinglian aversion to the Real Presence in the eucharist. How might Barnabas' response contribute to the discussion?

> What connection (if any) do you see between an extremely transcendent God (completely hidden) and the philosophy of mechanism? What corrective might be used to avoid the other end of the pendulum swing, that God's immanence, in the extreme, has Him manipulating/dabbling in every detail of life (yet taking into consideration Matt. 10:30)?

> Trypho's adoptionist view sounds as though it could have been a forerunner of the Latter Day Saint's elevation of men into gods and of much New Age thinking about humanity's ultimate destiny. What makes this view appealing to people of all ages, including today?

What traces of Docetism can be found today? How would you explain the phrase "God died" without falling into either Docetism or adoptionism?

What might be the benefits if Christians made greater use of Irenaeus' positioning of Jesus' life and work as part of the Third Article? How would this affect dialog between charismatic and non-charismatic Christians?

The difference between *messianic* and *wisdom* Christology corresponds to the question, What to emphasize: Jesus' divinity or His messianic fulfillment? The Old Roman Symbol and subsequent Apostles' Creed come down on the side of messianic fulfillment—probably in response to challenges from Marcion and the Gnostics. Compare the Apostles' to the Nicene Creed. Which responds most effectively to today's challenges to the faith? Why?

In what sense might some claim that Marcion prefigures dispensationalism? What connections exist between Gnosticism and New Age/Eastern philosophies? Comment on the claim that understanding the church's response to ancient heresies helps Christians today respond to contemporary challenges.

Ignatius and Irenaeus tied faith in the crucified-risen God-man Jesus to martyrdom. Justin Martyr tied faith to being a Christian missionary. What are the important connections for western civilization today (i.e., "the existential side of a Christ-confession")?

Chapter 4

Chapter 1 focuses on the uniqueness of the incarnation: that it did not have its roots in either Jewish or Hellenistic philosophy/mythology but (chapter 2) in Scripture's wisdom- and messianic-Christology. Chapter 3 shows that the apologetic for the incarnation continued to be necessary even through the second century after Christ. By the third century, the incarnation question moved from the basic "whether-or-not" to the refining question of "how"—the issues discussed in chapters 4–6. As background for the decisions of Nicea (chapter 5) and Chalcedon (chapter 6) and their normative definitions for today, chapter 4 presents the emphases of the West (basically messianic Christology) and the East (three variations of wisdom Christology).

Evaluate the necessity of *precise* explanations and terminology. Keep in mind that the events in this chapter were taking place amid great persecutions and martyrdom, when the basic existence of Christianity was at stake. What parallels do you see today?

If the credal phrase "for us men and for our salvation" influences how a believer answers the "whether-or-not" question, in what way does it also influence one's understanding of the "how" of the incarnation? [Relatedly, is "understanding the how" philosophically important to understanding and teaching the faith?]

Some Christians, using everyday terms, tend to think of the

Trinity (and, thus, Christ's divinity) in terms of modalism or three Gods—yet in this way affirming Jesus' divinity! Why should the church push for precision on this point?

How might a lack of understanding traditional precision be seen in, e.g., the Jehovah's Witnesses and the Latter Day Saints?

One of the reflection questions for chapter 3 asked, "How would you explain the phrase 'God died' without falling into either Docetism or adoptionism?" What additional insights in this chapter help answer that question?

Based on the church fathers' struggle to accurately describe the incarnation, comment on the merit of Mary's title, "Mother of God."

Behind the Nicene Creed's description of Jesus as "God of God, Light of Light" lie statements such as Tertullian's, "Even when the ray is shot from the sun, it is still part of the parent mass; the sun will still be in the ray, because it is a ray of the sun. There is no division of substance, but merely an extension."

How much should Christians today depend upon a pre-scientific explanation of (e.g.) sun and ray to describe the Trinity?

What Biblical alternatives would you suggest (if any)?

Chapter 5

If possible, try to sympathize with Arius' concern that the doctrines about Jesus should not detract from or conflict with doctrines about God. According to Skarsaune, Arius felt that (1) Alexander's phraseology allowed that God the Father was the one who died on the cross, and that (2) attempts to get around Alexander's folly relied on teaching that God's very nature was different after the incarnation than before.

What examples of error within contemporary Christianity have arisen when internal *logical* consistency is stressed (and Biblical doctrine is not upheld)?

How can philosophical integrity be maintained while striving for pure doctrine, just as it was at Nicea?

In chapter 4, Skarsaune explains the pre-Nicea definition of *hypostasis* as either (1) similar to the Latin *substantia*, the idea of *essence* (in distinction from a thing's attributes); or (2) the collective attributes by which a thing is known as an individual being. Arius evidently felt that, based on the first definition of *hypostasis*, his bishop was denying the oneness of God. The church responded at Nicea (as summarized here in chapter 5) by limiting *hypostasis* to its second meaning, and by using *ousia* (substance) to affirm God's oneness—thus retaining the time-honored term *hypostasis* (as well as maintaining the full place of Christ Jesus in the Trinity).

> How would you answer the charge that these distinctions are merely semantic gymnastics? Before answering, consider Skarsaune's point that Arius' views were "popular" and that the formulations of Nicea repeated the common Eastern "simple baptismal confession" rather than "a relatively detailed" confession of faith.

> Skarsaune suggests that Arius' problem stemmed not from a quibbling over terms but from his basic denial of the full divinity of Jesus as Wisdom, the emanation of God. How appropriate is it to evaluate people's overall orthodoxy on the basis of their Christology?

Skarsaune emphasizes that the Nicene Creed was not the product of state politics; yet it was Constantine's press for unity in the empire that occasioned it. Similar observations have been made for many of the great leaps forward in the visible church.

> Given the present fragmentation of the visible church and the challenges to it that vary by locale, what would it take for "a great leap forward" today?

> Strategically, Arius never had a chance; the house was stacked against him before the council doors even opened. Skarsaune justifies the politics of this by summarizing, "When the church confesses its faith, it does not at the same time question it." What, then, is the place of theological discussion to clarify doctrine (since the minority is not always wrong)?

How significant for today's systematics do you see the Cappadocian statement that Christ Jesus "take with Him the *whole* of us, for that which is not assumed is not saved"?

Chapter 6

The major theological positions (Antiochene, Alexandrian, and Ephesian) prior to Nicea, described in chapter 4, seem relatively differentiated. However, consider Skarsaune's descriptions of Theodore of Mopsuestia, c. 100 years post-Nicea: An Antiochene by birth; theologically with the Alexandrians (but not the Alexandrian Arius); but accused of standing with the Antiochene Paul of Samosata. (The previously "clean" positions of the three centers continue to reconfigure during the 100 years between Theodore and Chalcedon.)

Using a conclusion that, while labels are useful, the beliefs behind the labels may change over the years, how important is it for denominations today to maintain established terminology (e.g., as proof of their fidelity to the faith as previously defined)?

Under what circumstances should a denomination be in fellowship with another denomination with similar doctrine but differing terminology, and when should it insist on the same terminology?

Consider Skarsaune's observation concerning the Chalcedonian statement, that it served as "a necessary reminder for zealous disciples of Cyril" that his terminology was neither sacrosanct nor indispensable (skipping, for the moment, that it was not canonical either). Evaluate whether or not that observation should be applied to the formulations/terminology of any theologian.

Noting that "Chalcedon *opened up* the greatest Christological struggle in the Eastern church" rather than settling the issues, what are the caveats for doctrinal disputes over terms and their meanings?

Consider Skarsaune's points that (1) the Chalcedon expansion of the Nicene Creed was formulated to assist in teaching the faith to the common people, and (2) that the Chalcedon Definition was absorbed into the Athanasian Creed.

What challenges today might encourage the church to use the Nicene rather than the Apostles' Creed as its "popular" statement of faith?

The Athanasian Creed says of its formulations, "This is the catholic [universal] faith which, except a man believe faithfully and firmly, he cannot be saved." But to many contemporary "fisherfolk" (Skarsaune's phrase, quoting a bishop), it is not only God that is "one incomprehensible" but the Athanasian Creed itself. What place should this creed hold in teaching the faith to converts?

Postscript

Consider again some of the previous questions for reflection:

Some have held that the essence of Christianity does not require that the resurrection include a physical resuscitation of Jesus' body. In discussing that point, how might Skarsaune's line of thought be used?

Comment on the claim that understanding the church's response to ancient heresies helps Christians today respond to contemporary challenges.

Ignatius and Irenaeus tied faith in the crucified-risen God-man Jesus to martyrdom. Justin Martyr tied faith to being a Christian missionary. What are the important connections for western civilization today (i.e., "the existential side of a Christ-confession")?

Some Christians, using everyday terms, tend to think of the Trinity (and, thus, Christ's divinity) in terms of modalism or three Gods—yet in this way affirming Jesus' divinity! Why should the church push for precision on this point?

What place should the Nicene and/or Athanasian Creeds hold in teaching the faith to converts?

What, then, is the place of theological discussion?